THURSDAY'S CHILD:

MEMOIRS OF AN EX-NUN

by: Sue Potter

Published by **Washington House**
A division of Trident Media Company
801 N Pitt Street, Suite 123
Alexandria, VA 22314 USA

DEDICATION:

This book is dedicated in part to the fond memory of Sr. Clare Jerry who molded and educated me while passing on to me her profound philosophies and goals in life and who continues to watch over me from above. For all those who touched my life in Liberia especially those who perished in the civil war while I was there.

I also dedicate this book to my parents, the two wonderful people who gave me life and blessed that life with the joy and freedom for me to be who I am and what I want to be and who have been my main source of support, encouragement, and love.

CHAPTER ONE

Without warning, the school campus seemed to be surrounded by fighter jets dropping bombs and laden with soldiers who were shooting in every direction. Bullets and bombs were flying and falling all around us. The students hid under desks and chairs and some ran outside and hid under the trees in the schoolyard. I thought of raising a white flag or something to signal that we were innocent civilians attending school. I longed to go over to the junior section to see how Sister Doris and those over there were faring, but the firing was too heavy for me to risk crossing the courtyard. Instead I remained with my students and endured the terrified screams coming from within the walls of the junior school. A few of the braver students joined me on the corridor as, helplessly we watched the "shelling" of Greenville City.

As we stood there I felt the anger and fear rise to my throat. Sister Angela, Sister Doris, and I had to get out of there, and my one thought was how in heaven's name were we going to get out alive! The same excitement and enthusiasm that had gripped me five years ago when I was told that I was one of the four chosen to begin that mission to Liberia, West Africa, now gripped me to find a way out.

The jets kept circling the compound with such vengence I was now convinced that it was mistaken for something else. I paced the corridor rushing back and forth from each of the three classrooms making every effort to calm teachers and students. I wanted to ensure that not another one was going to run into the path of one of the bullets that flew in every direction. One too many of my students, five American nuns, and even the parish priest who had welcomed us to that mission had perished in the war. Instead of paralyzing me, the anger and fear motivated me to seek an end to this carnage. I was not going to lie down and die as easily as the others had!

The attack lasted for about an hour and just as suddenly as it had started, it ceased. For a few minutes no one moved. All senses were tuned for the horrendous sounds of the jets, and when they did not return, there was a mass exodus. Utter chaos reigned in the junior school as teachers as well as students jumped through windows and trampled each other as they rushed to get through the front door. I had no idea where Sister Doris was, and in the back of my head was the thought that Sister Angela had been killed by the bomb that seemed to have been dropped in the region of the convent and clinic.

Sheer confusion and stark fear were mirrored in the eyes of my high school teachers and students as I coaxed them out of their hiding places under the desks and chairs in the classrooms. Everyone, including myself, moved in zombie-like fashion. I managed to get everyone into one classroom, quickly said a short prayer, and dismissed them. I made them promise to keep close to the trees and bushes as they made their way to their homes. As they all left in one large group, I ran across the court-yard into the junior school in search of Sister Doris. The corri-dor was completely deserted and silent as I ran its length to the last classroom, which was Sister's.

There I found her, visibly shaken but holding up coura-geously for the group of students and the few teachers gathered around her. They were praying the rosary, and as they finished the frightened and shaken group left to make their way home. I told her that the students and I had seen a bomb land in the area of the convent, and neither of us at that moment could voice the fear that closed around our hearts. I stayed with her as she locked up the building, then we proceeded to the high school where I collected my handbag, locked my office, and we left.

We took a short cut through the bushes to reach the convent which was about a mile from the school compound. Neither of us spoke. I could not tell what Sister was thinking but amidst the confusion, hurt, and anger I was experiencing two questions clearly emerged, "How did I end up in this hot zone?" and, "How am I going to get out?"

As my thoughts roamed, they wandered back to that day in August 1989 when I was told by the superior, Sister Jane, that I was one of the sisters chosen to pioneer our newest mission to Liberia, West Africa. No one knew who was to be sent and several sisters volunteered but we were told that four sisters would be chosen and sent. One day I had to take one of the sisters to see Sister Jane on business. As I sat in the parlor to wait until their meeting was over, Sister Jane came in and closed the door. My eyes popped, uncertain as to what I had done to deserve a reprimand, but she only smiled warmly as she sat down and took my hands in hers.

"Sister, how would you like to go to Liberia?" she asked. "I would love to!" I replied exuberantly. "Well, you are one of those chosen to go," she announced. I tried to find out who the other three were but she wouldn't tell me and instead made me promise not to tell anyone until she had called a general meeting to formally announce who would be sent. I thanked her profusely because I was so happy and excited. As Sister Jane got up to leave she gave me a book to read. It was about the presence of the Church in Liberia and contained all the history about the country.

Liberia was the farthest place from my mind at this time. When I was studying Africa in high school geography I was strangely fascinated by the continent, then, when Trinidad was undergoing political and racial upheavals in 1970, I had dreamed that one day my mother and I had gone shopping when we were caught up in a sea of people of African descent and could find no way out. Suddenly, out of nowhere, this very tall young man with a low afro haircut emerged, took our hands, and led us across the street to safety. This dream remains vivid in my mind to this very day because I actually met the person who saved us

7

in my dream! But though I had those significant connections to Africa I had no thoughts about Liberia because I had never really heard of the country until the name was brought up in my religious community.

I learned that Liberia is the oldest African independent state and is situated on the western coast of Africa, traditionally called the "Grain Coast." It is bordered by Sierra Leone on the west, the Ivory Coast on the east, and Guinea on the north. Liberia's Atlantic coast stretches 354 miles between Cape Mount in the north and Cape Palmas in the South. There are fifteen main rivers, the Cavalla and St. Paul being the most important. The climate, warm all year round, has marked wet and dry seasons. The wet or "rainy" season is between November or December to April or May, and maximum rainfall occurs in June and September.

The total area of land which forms this country is 37,743 square miles and the population at that time (1989) was 2,200,000. The official language of the country is English, but the fabric of its culture is embroidered with the mother tongue or "dialect" of each of the various ethnic groups. The economy is largely agricultural, but minerals account for most of Liberia's earnings. Rice and cassava, the staple food crops, are locally produced and consumed. Rubber, coffee, and timber are the main export crops, and the vast development of these industries provides many jobs in the rural areas where they are situated.

Liberia became independent on July 26, 1847, as a small republic of immigrant black Americans. Before the immigration, the largely forested area was peopled by various ethnic groups that form the overwhelming majority of the population today. The most important of these are the Kpelle, Bassa, Kru, Vai, Krahn, and Mandingo. The Krus can be found mainly in the eastern region and are important for their agricultural and fishing skills. It is said that the Krus know the rivers and connecting ocean like the back of their hands. They boast that none of their members were ever sold or taken into slavery because they formed a pact with the slave-ship owners and navigators to assist them to find their way out of the waters after they had conducted their trade.

When the slave trade ended, many of the freed slaves from the United States of America emigrated to Liberia. Thus when the republic came into existence under President J.J. Roberts, its constitution was based on that of the United States. Emigration to Liberia continued, and the 20,000 black Americans who found their way there by 1866, were joined by a group of West Indians, including a large contingent from Barbados. Even though the number of Americo-Liberians was small, they fought constantly for over a century with the local Liberians whom they called "tribesmen." Even within the Americo-Liberians there was a power struggle between the "mulattos" (those of partial white birth) and those of pure African descent. President J.J. Roberts was himself the leading member of the "mulattos" who conquered and subjected the locals or tribesmen of the interior of Liberia. This caused frequent outbursts or revolts.

In 1944 William V.S. Tubman succeeded J.J. Roberts as President and made great strides to reduce the discrimination and hostility between the Americo-Liberians and the local Liberians or tribesmen. The locals were given political rights and opportunities for education but discrimination and oppression were still rampant. However, President Tubman's efforts to promote modernization in Liberia as well as reunification between the two groups, had their limits. Upon his death, his successor, William Tolbert, continued some of President Tubman's policies. Corruption reigned among government officials and Tolbert endeavored to stamp it out. He showed genuine concern for the ordinary people and made great strides in improving life for them. He strengthened relations with the U.S. and other foreign nations and was characterized by his firmness and sense of justice. Yet, despite his efforts to bring about equality for all Liberians, the inherited inequalities were still great and largely contributed to the unrest which grew in 1979 and escalated into a coup in 1980 when, on April 12, troops led by the government army seized power in Monrovia. There was little bloodshed but President Tolbert was killed by the rebel soldiers.

Master Sergeant Samuel K. Doe, the 28-year-old national commanding Officer of the Krahn ethnic group, took command of the government and became the twenty-first head of state of Liberia and the first indigenous national to hold that office. He spent the next few days speaking of the "rampant corruption" and violation of human rights to justify the coup. He promised a society based on justice and human dignity. In 1981, he was commissioned commander-in-chief of the armed forces. All civilian members of government were made army officers and civilian ministers were made majors. Later on he made himself army general. Everyone was not happy with this highly military regime and in 1985 an attempt was made to overthrow it. Tension mounted, and against this background Doe was declared president in 1986.

Economic crises and oppression grew. Everyone had come to recognize that the very thing Doe had set out to eradicate, he had instead encouraged and supported. He filled official positions with his own countrymen (people of the Krahn tribe to which he belonged) whether they were qualified for the position or not. He amassed enormous bank accounts worldwide and continuously built mansions in various of the country's thirteen counties. If anyone dared question or challenge him or his actions, he had them discreetly "removed." So much for justice and human rights!

As I learned about this colorful but troubling background of Liberia, my spirits were not daunted because I felt that we were not going to be affected by the politics of the country. We were going to do God's work, teaching and training the people to live better lives, and we had no intentions of becoming involved in any other business unless it directly interfered with our work. How wrong I was!

I was brought out of my reverie by Sister Doris who all this time had been walking silently with me. We had almost reached the convent and had not come up with any answers. Sister then declared very determinedly: "We have to get out of this place. If we stay here we will be killed. We must get out!" I couldn't agree more but I had no idea how.

CHAPTER TWO

I was born on Thursday, September 2, the first of seven children to bless the lives of Sebastien and Runesia. My parents are both the great-grandchildren of Indian immigrants who were brought to the country of Trinidad in the West Indies as indentured laborers after the slave trade ended. My mother, Runesia, is from a well-to-do family and is an only child of Hindu parents although she has thirteen aunts and uncles and over fifty first cousins.

My father, Sebastien, born into a more humble background, is one of seventeen children born to Hindu parents. A few of his siblings born before him either died at birth or did not live more than a few weeks or months. When my father was born, his mother was told that if she wanted him to survive she would have to abide by a certain Hindu custom, she had to "sell" this baby to someone of a different religion, preferably a Christian, for something other than money.

Thus my father was "sold" for a pound of salt to the caretaker of the Catholic Church who became his godmother, when she had him baptized in the church. She raised my father to be a good and God-fearing person and gave him back to his family when he was twelve years old. As he grew, his mother gave birth to three more children who survived and are still alive. My father and mother were brought together by his second sister, Carmen, who knew my mother through her mother. My mother was sixteen, and when her mother died shortly after, she and Sebastien were married and I was born exactly one year after their wedding day.

From a very early age I was exposed to books and I grew to be an avid reader and an ardent storyteller. While my father loved to tell us stories about his childhood, which seemed so exciting and colorful, my mother preferred to read to her kids. One verse she never tired of reciting to us was:

"Monday's child is fair of face, Tuesday's child is full of grace; Wednesday's child is full of woe, Thursday's child has far to go; Friday's child ...."

When I could barely form the words I would ask my mother what day I was born on and she always replied, "Thursday, sweetie." "And what is Thursday's child, Mummy?" I would ask. In a solemn tone of voice and with a wistful expression, she would reply, "Thursday's child has far to go." Her expression made me feel as if she could read into my future. I guess to a certain extent, she was aware of certain things only she was privileged to know.

When a child is born to a Hindu family, the date and time of birth is written down on a piece of paper and given to someone, usually the child's father, to take to the family pundit (priest). He reads this information and then consults the huge sacred book only he can read and interpret. First he names the child (my Hindu name has thirteen letters, and up to this day, I cannot pronounce it), then he notes certain significant occurrences, both good and bad, that will take place in this child's life. These he writes down for the child's mother only to read. She keeps these things sealed in her heart and will endeavor to offer prayers and sacrifices to protect her child from the bad or evil influences that may surround him or her.

My mother always said to me that I was born to do great things and reach far places. I never understood where she thought I'd go but I didn't question her. As a child, I felt that my mother (and father) knew everything. She is a devout Hindu and her deep faith in her religion makes her a very prayerful, good, and kind person. Even though I never embraced Hinduism myself, and therefore did not always understand the teachings and practices of this religion, I have great respect for my mother's devotion and the job she's done as a mother and a homemaker. My father, on the other hand, has been the tower of strength and discipline in my life. A physically large person, no one dared defy or challenge him in any way. He is a man of few words, but when we were kids, if we were misbehaving and got that "look" from him we generally knew what would follow. He was no advocate of "spare the rod and spoil the child." He has, however, mellowed with age and now proudly reflects on his efforts at successfully bringing up seven kids.

The house where I grew up was simple and modest but I have happy memories of the time spent there. It sat on an acre of land fenced around by hibiscus shrubs well over four feet tall. There was ample space all around the building for us to play and we had to take turns sweeping, pulling up grass, and keeping the area tidy. Though we were not Christians, we celebrated Christmas in all the splendor with which we celebrated Divali, the Hindu equivalent of Christmas. Several of the smells of the various foods my mother prepared for us and other things done in anticipation of the celebration of Christmas Day still linger in my mind. Christmas Eve day was when the ham was boiled and baked; the fruit cakes, butter sponge cakes, and coconut sweet bread were baked; and the different drinks like mauby, ginger beer, and sorrel were boiled and bottled.

There was no electricity in the house so there was no refrigerator or electric hand mixer or electric stove. An empty five-gallon cooking oil can was procured for boiling the leg of pork which would soon become our Christmas ham. The entire top of the can was removed, then it was thoroughly scoured, filled with water, and set on the outdoor fire. This fire was made by first setting in a safe spot in the yard three concrete blocks to form a "U" shape, then filling the inside space with dried twigs and logs which were lit and fanned with newspaper to coax out the flames. Once this got going my mother concentrated on getting the coal pot lit and the coals burning at just the right temperature to accommodate the drum oven for baking the cakes.

While she was tending to that chore I would be set on a chair with a big bowl of butter and sugar and a wooden spoon on my lap. The task was mine to manually blend these two ingredients to a perfect cream. While I did this the other kids ran around and played and every so often one of them escaped and ran to the bowl for a lick of the soft, sweet cream. When I had a perfect cream and felt as if my arm would drop off, my mother would relieve me of it and then divide it up for the different batters she was going to prepare. The next time I would see the batter bowls was when my mother had poured the batters into the cake pans and then beckoned us to "lick the bowls."

Preparations went well into the night and when all the cooking was done it was then time to "dress" the house. The "Morris" chairs had been given the sandpaper and varnish treatment days before so the house was permeated with the sweet smell of new varnish and adding to this on Christmas Eve night was the new linoleum placed on the floor, the new oilcloth placed on the dining room table and finally the crisp, new curtains on the two doors and four windows. I cherish many happy childhood memories in that house but Christmas was one of the happiest.

I can still remember the toys and new clothes we received. Even though my parents were not rich, they somehow always managed to provide the best for us. We were not allowed to go to others children's homes to play, but our friends could come and play with us. However, since my father had the reputation of being very strict and was critical of anyone who came to visit us, I refrained from bringing home any of the few friends I had. A few years later when I was fifteen a businessman in the area bought out the block on which we lived to build a factory, and my parents were given a plot of land at the end of the street, which was along the main road. Here my parents built a bigger, more modern and comfortable house and this is where they still reside.

As I was growing up, my father was one of the few people

in our village who owned a car. This made me the object of both envy and admiration among friends and neighbors. Every Sunday afternoon my parents would pack the seven of us kids in the car and take us for a drive to a different part of the country. I strongly believe this was the beginning of my love for traveling and appreciation of the beauty of my country. My mother's parents both died before she was sixteen years old, but my father's were still alive and lived in a village in the deep south of the country, so at least once a month we visited them.

I loved this village called Carapichima and looked forward to those visits. In my grandparents' yard were a number of fruit trees, and I remember one year, they produced so abundantly that in my fourteen-year-old mind, they seemed to bear only for me. I tore many a dress and scraped my arms and legs climbing to retrieve these fruits, but the pain was worth the admiration and the happiness of those who shared the fruits. These visits ended when I was twenty and my father's parents died, within months of each other.

From a very young age I assumed a lot of responsibility for my family. My parents both worked tirelessly to build up their business and provide a comfortable life for us all. My father loved cars and after working for many years with a large company he was able to start his own business. My mother loved working with flowers and after taking a few courses she ventured out marketing her skills at flower making and arranging both fresh and artificial flowers. While she was an excellent homemaker, as the eldest child I was expected to do my part, and much of the care of my four sisters and two brothers was bestowed upon me. Even though it was a burden at times, I could not go out and play with other children as I would have liked, and so I never had a lot of friends, I generally enjoyed caring for Marlene, Maureen, Reena, Junior, Judy, and baby David.

As I grew up and questioned the origin of our names, my mother told me that since she and my father were such ardent movie fans they named us girls after famous movie stars - yes, I was actually named after Marilyn Monroe! Since Junior was the first boy after four girls he was named after my father; and David, whom I treasure in a special way, was named after the biblical David. When he was born, I was at the age when I felt that I knew everything (on the threshold of teenagehood). I was attending Sunday School and learning all about David and Goliath. I was fascinated with the character of David and told my Mom that if her baby was a boy, he was definitely going to be a "David" so "David" he was promptly named when I saw him a few hours after his birth. I love all my siblings equally in a passionate and protective way. We enjoyed playing "dress up" in our parents' clothes and imitating them. One evening my father went out and my mother was busy in the kitchen so the seven of us gathered in one bedroom to play. The elder of my two brothers, Junior, was about five at the time. He was very chubby and had long curls that reached down to his shoulders. He had a violent temper and a sharp tongue which was always getting him into trouble.

He dressed in my father's favorite shirt, stuck a cigarette in his mouth (my father was a heavy smoker), got on one of the beds, and proceeded to act and speak just like my father. We were jumping up and down on the other beds and laughing our heads off and so were quite unaware that my father had returned and was standing by the door silently taking in the whole scene. My mother had joined him and only when she coughed and we looked up did we see my father. First we froze, then we scampered to avoid punishment, but to our surprise my father did not holler or reach for his belt. He just gave us one of his rare, precious smiles and turned away.

My mother said that from the time I could talk, I was always asking: "But why Mummy?" to everything she said, and since she hadn't all the answers, she decided early that I should go to school. Thus at age four I attended a private nursery school run by Mrs. Davis in her home. She was the very first person of a different race I was encountering and immediately I noticed the difference, my question to her was, "Why are you different?" She used that opportunity to tell the class a beautiful story of God's great love of his people and his desire to create a peaceful and interesting world. "That's why," she explained, "He made so many different types of people." Mrs Davis made a great impression on my life and I went home at noon each day singing her praises to my parents. She was well on in age, and not long after I moved on to elementary school she passed away.

Elementary school days were a blast for me. I was a regular tomboy, and as this was a coed school I preferred to hang out with the boys rather than the girls who were always gossiping or making confusion among themselves. Corporal punishment was allowed in this school, and I received my fair share of it because I was always getting into fights by standing up to bullies. My hair was extremely long and my mother would not allow me to comb it in any other fashion but two plaits with ribbons at the ends.

One day, Cecil, the class bully, who sat behind me, tied the ends of the ribbons to the chair. When I attempted to rise to answer a question, I found myself tied to the chair and everyone laughed their heads off. Greatly humiliated, I reached over and threw my hardest punch into Cecil's face. It caught him on the nose and soon blood was dripping down his shirt. The teacher sent me to the principal who punished me with five strokes on my palms with a tamarind rod. I was sent to detention for the rest of the class and got home late after walking the mile to my home.

As I neared our front gate who did I see standing there but the despicable, cowardly, Cecil and his mother. He was still wearing his blood-stained shirt and seemed to have told my parents a very tall tale from the grim looks I saw on their faces. My father said that he would have to punish me for fighting in school and then for coming home late. I just went berserk. I began to shout and scream that it was not fair and that no one was interested in listening to both sides of the story.

My mother managed to quieten me and said, "There are two sides to every coin, so let us hear her side of what happened." Cecil glared at me because he knew that after I was finished telling the truth he would be in a lot of trouble. I told the adults what had really happened and how the principal had punished me unfairly. When I was finished, my mother was so angry she turned to Cecil and his mother and drove them out of our front yard. As they left, Cecil's mother dragged him off by the ear and kept shouting how she was going to punish him when they got home.

At age eleven, after taking a national examination, I won a full scholarship to attend the very exclusive, highest-rated girls' high school in my country. My parents and teachers expressed their pride, but that did not alleviate the nervousness and lack of confidence I felt in attending that school. In elementary school, I was the smartest, tallest, prettiest, most popular girl, but now all these qualities were challenged. There were girls of every different ethnic, economical, and social background. As the years passed I grew into a very lanky, awkward teenager. I did well in my studies but I did not have many friends and felt intimidated by some of my class peers who were bossy and snobbish. I did my best to ignore them, but they still got to the more timid students.

The highest-ranked all boys' school in the country was our "brother" school, and while there were strict rules about speaking to the boys (the boys' school was about a mile away from our school and a lot of us took the train to and from school) there were ample opportunities for us to fraternize with them. Many of the girls had boyfriends in that school. In my senior year, I had a huge crush on Jason, also a senior.

I saw him every Tuesday when both schools competed in chess tournaments, every Thursday when we met for debate team practice, and every morning, when he walked to his school from the train station. But I was so shy that I never said one word to him. I later learned that he was the steady boyfriend of the prefect of my class who was a sweet and kind girl. I was glad it was she, and I quickly gave up my secret feelings for Jason.

After graduating from high school at age seventeen, I told my father I wanted a break from studies before going to college or seeking a job. I stayed at home for almost a year. I helped my mother with my small brothers and sisters, and with housework, but I began to grow restless. My father soon found me a job working at the <u>Trinidad Guardian</u>, the top newspaper in my country.

One of his classmates was the accountant there, so I filled in for the payroll clerk who was on maternity leave. That meant that the job was only for three months, but since it was my first ever job, I gave it my all and did the best I could. When Mrs. Lee returned she was impressed with what I had accomplished (setting files in order, balancing accounts, and cleaning up a lot of stuff that had piled up). She asked for me to stay on at least another month to help her as much as I could. I was sad to leave when the time came but I had learned a lot there, especially from Mrs. Lee.

My mother tried her best to persuade me to study nursing but my mind was set on teaching. I sat for the teachers' exam and passed so I applied to teach in the public school system as well as in private schools. When I didn't get any positive responses, I sent out applications for clerical positions, and within a month, I was doing cylinder control for a company that marketed commercial gas in cylinders. After two years there, I got a letter from the nun who was in charge of the home for mentally handicapped children in the country. I was mystified and felt that letter was significant.

I decided to confide in Sylvia, the secretary to the president of the company. When I showed her the letter she immediately said that I should go for the interview and accept the position that was offered me. She confided that something was amiss, but she couldn't divulge details. I went the next day for the interview, and while the nun explained that the salary would be half of what I was now receiving, the teaching position available was mine. Without hesitation, I told her that I would accept. Very discreetly the next day I sought Sylvia and told her the outcome of my interview. Only then did she reveal that the company was selling out to its competitor. In a week's time employees would be offered either sums of compensation or junior positions with the new company. When the time came, I accepted the severance pay offered and looked forward to my new career in educating the borderline mentally handicapped.

From the moment I entered the compound that housed dormitories, a school for the handicapped children, and a convent for the seven nuns who cared for these children, I knew my life was going to be transformed. It was just a gut feeling. Many of these children were also physically handicapped and abandoned at birth, hence the dormitories were overflowing for the nuns kept accepting children whose parents did not know how to care for them and wanted to save themselves the embarrassment of having a handicapped child. As I began to teach my group, I was in turn being taught and soon discovered a lot of things about myself.

Within my family we knew that our parents cared for us and we loved each other, but we were not physically demonstrative. Here at the institution, hugs were freely given and accepted. I soon grew to look beyond the slurred speech, the rivers of drool, the unsteady steps, and to embrace these loving and lovable human beings with a suppressed love which they had gently stroked and drawn out of me. I was twenty years old, very single, and extremely shy and reserved. In my previous jobs, I went through the motions of doing a job because I needed the money. Now, with these kids and in the presence of the nuns, I found immense joy and contentment in what I was doing.

The journey to and from the institution was particularly tedious taking over an hour but I never complained. I grasped at every opportunity to spend extra time with the children and the nuns. I took several courses studying and specializing in

"Special Education," thus allowing me to be more capable of dealing with my special kids. Despite my shyness I soon became fast friends with Ann, Helen, and Shelly who taught me to "hang out," to guzzle beer and to smoke cigarettes. I also befriended Sister Kathy, one of the nuns, and as I spoke to her and the others and observed them, I found myself drawn to their lifestyle.

CHAPTER THREE

The house where sisters or nuns live is called a convent. They live in groups of at least three and these are called communities. The lives of religious sisters are very structured, disciplined, and centered around prayer and imitating the life of Jesus. I was not a Catholic but I made every effort to attend Mass at the convent before going to teach my class. Each time I witnessed the celebration of this service, a hunger to share the passion of this religion grew in me as well as a deep desire to partake of that "Community Life" that was the Sisters'.

After receiving religious instructions from one of the sisters, I became a member of the Catholic Church. I became very active in my community as I participated in various Church groups and activities. My mother knew that I intended to become a nun and tried her best to dissuade me. She tried to arrange dates for me. I assured her that I had no problem with men but I felt deep down that God was calling me to something in life other than getting married and having children, as was expected of me as the eldest child of a Hindu family. When my mother saw my determination she did her best to ensure that I was well prepared. I had to have medical and psychological testing, special clothes made, and, most important, I had mentally and emotionally to prepare myself for this new life I was about to embrace.

Within one year of becoming a Catholic I entered the convent on January 6th. This is a special day of remembrance in the Catholic Church, the Feast of the Epiphany when the Three Kings visit the Infant Jesus bringing him gifts from their kingdoms. It was a very simple ceremony of reception attended by the various superiors of the order and the sisters living in that community. The only member of my family that accompanied me was my mother. She cried her heart out throughout, and later on the sister who gave her a lift back home told me that she felt that she was not going to see me ever again, but she was assured that I had not entered one of those convents where the nuns are locked away from the world.

This convent served as "Mother House" (where the general superior and her councilors lived), Novitiate (where the novice mistress and all those in training lived) as well as an asylum for old, sick, visiting sisters, as well as those who were too difficult to fit in any of the other communities. It was built upon a virgin mountain and sat humbly at the feet of the Regional Seminary (where young men were trained for the priesthood), which was one level up. It was the monastery for monks which majestically graced the top of the mountain. The monastery was built by the monks who came from Holland as well as other parts of Europe. Then they set about constructing a road for the hundreds of faithful who flocked to the church daily to seek the prayers of the monks.

I entered the convent a few years after Vatican II hence there was tremendous upheaval, (both good and bad), in the Church. There were changes that included modification of religious habits (the special garb worn by religious sisters, brothers, and priests). These changes were drastic enough to allow the sisters to throw off the religious habits completely and wear regular secular clothes. This caused great rifts and pockets of resentment within religious orders and among communities between those who refused to modify or change the habit and those who grasped at the most radical changes.

The particular religious order I had entered had been extremely strict, and when they refused to relax some their rules, there was a great exodus. The superiors maintained pre-Vatican customs and therefore failed to attract vocations for many years, so when I entered I was the only postulant for that two-year period of training (the first stage of becoming a nun where one is accepted into the community but is treated more like an observer).

The sisters centered and shaped their lives around liturgy, prayer, and simple living. I was taught that religious sisters should endeavor to be perfect in whatever they were doing. Everything had to be done perfectly even though, as human beings, we were not perfect. The sisters prayed the psalms four times a day (the Liturgy of the Hours). This symbolic act of chanting or singing certain assigned psalms is an emulation of and a joining with the choirs in heaven who sing the praises of God unceasingly.

There were times when I was so deeply engrossed in the task I was performing, whether sweeping the chapel, cleaning toilets, preparing supper for the community, gardening or attending Novitiate classes, when the bell for prayer was rung. I would be upset at having my activity disrupted and would go to the chapel disturbed and distracted. What I often discovered as I began to chant the psalms was that my thoughts and emotions would be calmed by the psalms, which expressed how I was feeling at that particular time.

I had always felt that the psalmists had nothing in common with me, the dilemmas with which I was faced or the world in which I lived. Yet here I realized that they empathized with me, allowing me to face my feelings and deal with them. I discovered that I was frequently angry but I managed to successfully suppress these feelings and deal later with them as I recited the psalms. Some of them are laced with anger and violence, for example, Psalm 39. Verses 2-3 state:

"The prosperity of the wicked stirred my grief, my heart burned within me,At the thought of it the fire blazed up and my tongue burst into speech..."

Although it seems that judgment is being passed by calling someone wicked, actually the anger is directed towards God. This consoled me immensely, and I was able to channel my anger through ways God made possible, gardening, playing various musical instruments, singing, art, and simply praying instead of wanting to lash out at those who had made me angry.

I giggled and laughed a lot in the Novitiate and I soon realized why. My days were rigidly structured and I was required to do things I had never done before. Thus to relieve the tension and stress caused by this rigidity, I learned to laugh instead of bottling it up. The superior often advocated that it was necessary to have a sense of humor in order to persevere in religious life so I cultivated mine. Each member of the community had to take turns preparing the Liturgy of the Hours and while some stuck to the traditional monotones chant, a few more adventurous ones interspersed the session with drama, singing, and even dancing.

There was one particular sister who was well over sixty years of age but was very unconventional. When her turn came to plan the liturgy, one never knew what to expect. Some of the sisters didn't go to chapel for her sessions but prayed quietly in their rooms. As a junior sister I had no choice so I went and thoroughly enjoyed whatever performance sister had to offer. Most times I couldn't say my line or verse because I had dissolved in giggles.

At the end of the two years as a postulant I had to petition to the superiors to become a novice in the order. This is the second stage, when one is given a modified version of the religious habit to wear as well as more responsibilities in the community in preparation of professing the three vows of poverty (denouncing ownership of wealth and choosing to share everything in community); chastity (renouncing the right to marry and have a family); and obedience (becoming selfless, and totally obedient to the superior who represented Christ).

This stage of religious life is the real time of testing to see if a young woman does have a religious vocation and is sincere in her desires to become a nun. I realized that many of the older sisters thought it was their duty to make life miserable for me, even the sister who was responsible for my training (she was given the title of novice mistress). As a novice I was not permitted to go out to classes or to serve in any of the other communities, neither was I allowed to visit home and stay overnight. During this two-year period I experienced profound loneliness and spiritual dryness which no amount of praying or spiritual reading could cure.

My special charge was a sister confined to a wheelchair who seemed to want to live to be as old as Moses. She was sweet and kind but she was also very trying. Since I was the lowliest member of the community it was my responsibility to look after her. When there was a community outing and she couldn't or wouldn't go, that meant I didn't either. I didn't mind that at all but what I did mind a whole lot was the unfairness and unkindness of the other sisters because I was not of their rank. There was one particular older nun who was wicked and unkind. She was one of the councilors of the superior and she used this position of power to scare the younger, junior sisters. She loved to gossip and carry news and never had anything good to say about anybody.

Whenever I confronted the novice mistress she would tell me that these were examples to aid in my sanctification and I should learn serious lessons from them. There was also one superior who did everything in her power to discourage me from becoming close friends with any of the sisters. She said that religious life should teach me to "make sacrifices," that is, to forego earthly, personal pleasures so that I would grow to be holy like Jesus. I felt that the sacrifice concept was going too far when on the two separate occasions when my sisters Maureen and Marlene got married I could not attend the ceremonies because I was in retreat. I cried, screamed in anger at God, and then when I was totally spent I simply prostrated myself before the crucifix and prayed my heart out for my sisters and my family.

I suffered silently and found much solace in taking long walks into the mountains. During these times I would experience a great oneness with God and nature. There was a deep peace in my soul and a fulfilling sense that God did want me to be a nun and would not abandon me. That knowledge was very comforting and gave me the joy and strength to cope with any situation, no matter how tough or challenging, or any grumpy, evil or old sister who crossed my path.

I took temporary or first vows in the order but I still was not given any significant assignment. I longed to go out and serve on the missions but I was still residing at the Mother House because I was the only junior sister so a lot of the menial community tasks were still mine. A sister remains in temporary vows until she feels and the community judges that she is ready to make these vows more permanent. She therefore renews her vows every year and can do so for up to nine years. She can make her final profession within that time but after the nine years if her mind is not made up then some serious decisions are made concerning her religious vocation.

After my second year as a junior sister the superior said to me very offhandedly one day: "Well, Sister, since you are not going off to the missions, maybe we can send you to the seminary to study!" I was offended by her attitude but in an effort to be a good, humble, and holy nun, I graciously accepted her offer. Our regional seminary is also the faculty of theology of the University of the West Indies located in Trinidad, thus one can read for a degree in theology by studying at the seminary. It was decided that I would do exactly that and that was exactly what my soul needed at that particular time in my life.

I studied four years of psychology, a subject I thoroughly enjoyed, I studied the bible from cover to cover, I entered into the world of famous philosophers and theologians and learned things that tested and tried my faith, beliefs, and philosophies in life. I also made very important and lasting friendships with many of the young men who came from all the different islands of the Caribbean to study for the priesthood. I became a member of the respected seminary choir and took part in concerts and dramatic presentations. The year of my graduation, the seminary celebrated its twenty-fifth anniversary and there was a week-long period of activities. One significant event was the presentation of an award-winning play written by a man who had been the first young man to set foot in the seminary when it opened its doors.

Unfortunately he did not persevere in his desire to become a priest and after leaving the seminary he became the country's leading playwright. Since there were parts cast for women in this play, and a few of us studying at the seminary at the time, I tried out for one. It was for the part of a prostitute but it was soon decided that I didn't have what it took to portray a prostitute I was given instead the role of the thirteen-year-old girl, Esther, who was the one source of hope in the broken situation the play represented.

I had to get special permission from the superior to remove my habit and veil and wear secular clothes in public. She gave me the necessary permission, but my actions did not go down well with a few of the sisters. That did not deter me, and soon I learned that once what I was doing was not a crime or hurting anyone, I did not let people's opinions, especially those of some of the nuns who were considered hypocrites, deter me.

While studying at the seminary I had also embarked upon studies for diplomas in teaching. Thus after graduating from the seminary with a degree in theology I was better qualified and capable at teaching all levels. I felt that I was ready to make that final commitment, so I petitioned to the Superior and her councilors to be allowed to make my Final profession of vows in the religious order. I had my qualms because I felt that I had isolated myself by standing up for myself, for speaking out against things I didn't agree with, and for befriending those that were ostracized. I prayed fervently that God's will be done, but I wasn't afraid. I told God that if he wanted me to remain a nun he would provide the way, and he sure did because I received the necessary votes that made me eligible to become a "senior sister."

Early in the gospel of St. John, Jesus turns to two young men who were following him and asks them: "What do you seek?" "Where do you live?" they in turn ask. "Come and see," Jesus replies. When a sister makes her perpetual profession of the three vows, she is confronted with the same question: "What do you seek?" Responses vary among the different religious communities, but basically it is: "I ask that I may follow Christ and persevere in this community until death." The ceremony of a sister professing final vows is very grand, full of rituals and symbolism, and is witnessed by family members and friends who are specially invited for the occasion.

I was already clothed in the religious habit when I professed temporary vows. The habit of this particular order consisted of a simple brown tunic held by a narrow band on which a huge rosary is hung. A white bib or wimple is worn around the neck, and over that a yoke-shaped scapular, the same length as the tunic, is fastened at the shoulders with invisible pins. To complete the ensemble, a shoulder length black veil covers the head. It is held securely in place by a thin metal or plastic bandeau which was threaded through a fold at the front end of the material.

As signs of my final profession of vows, I was given a long silver chain with a medal bearing the symbol of that particular order, and the archbishop placed a gold ring bearing the same symbol upon the ring finger of my right hand. A sister professing final vows must choose a motto and a title. As my motto I chose: "Thy Will Be Done." This was inscribed on the inside of the ring But since there were so many words and my ring was so tiny, the motto was condensed to "Fiat" which in Latin, expresses the same thing. My title, "Sr ..... of the Agony of Jesus," was inscribed at the back of the medal on the chain.

One other symbolic action was when the superior pinned a floor-length black silk veil on my head. It fell like a shroud around me and the only other time I would wear this would be at my burial. Finally, as a sign of a total giving of myself to God, I had to sing aloud the verse chosen by the superiors of this order: "Uphold me O Lord by your promise and I shall live, do not disappoint me in my hope." I now joined the ranks of professed sisters and continued my life as a regular nun in various of the communities, teaching and working with groups of young people on weekend retreats.

Along with all the other religious orders, the order to which I belonged was seeking to conquer new grounds so upon the invitation of the bishop there, we were asked to begin a mission in Liberia, West Africa. The country was first visited by the superiors who then met to decide who would be chosen to pioneer the mission. That religious order also had missions throughout the Caribbean, England, and the United States. I had visited and worked in all of them. During my three-month summer break from university I would volunteer to replace the sisters who worked on these missions so that they could visit their families or go on vacations they deserved.

I was very close to Sister Emma, the regional superior of the order who had also trained me in the final stage in the novitiate. She was a very practical, down-to-earth person, but she was not very popular. Sisters feared or disliked her because they experienced the fury of her temper when they behaved stupidly or stepped out of line. She loved the sisterhood and our particular order with a fierceness that scared the sisters who did not know her. While she trained me I learned many lessons that have supported me through life. She was full of wisdom and always imparted some important lesson with a story.

Living and working closely with her I was able to see through her charade. She reminded me so much of myself. Her physical strength was a cover-up for her physical and emotional weaknesses, and the immense pain that marked her life but to which she never surrendered. I was able to break through her tough exterior by being gentle and nonjudgmental. Soon the superiors recognized that I worked well with Sister Emma and so along with all my other duties I was given the joyous task of caring for her. She was always ill and was often at death's door but did not want anyone "babying" her, and I knew how to handle her. She grew to trust me unreservedly and I was allowed to handle confidential matters for her. I became her chauffeur, nurse, and general assistant in any project she undertook, while she in turn became my best friend and mentor.

Sister Emma was a very gifted and talented individual who knew no bounds in helping others. With exquisite deftness she taught me to ice cakes so that I was able single-handedly to produce a three-layered wedding cake for my brother and his bride as well as elaborate birthday cakes for my nieces. From her I learned to prepare gourmet meals of any nationality, and sew garments fit for a queen.

Under her tutorship I learned to play the guitar, flute, piano, and organ, to develop my artistic skills, and to achieve much more so that I could appreciate the fullness of life. I spent altogether ten years under her skillful mastership, and at the end of that period I was well prepared to be a perfect housekeeper, or hostess to a president or successful businesswoman. Under her spiritual guidance I had deepened my prayer life to such an extent that I now truly believed in the power of prayer and the great things it could achieve once God was approached with deep faith and humility.

Ever since the day I found her passed out cold on the floor in the chapel, whenever she was gone for long I would go in search of her. One day I went to her office to check if she was all right. I found her on the couch in the corner of the room very distressed over an official document that lay open on her lap. I didn't ask any questions but just sat at her feet as I often did when I saw her distressed. After a while I got up to leave and she asked me to get the car out of the garage and run an errand to the Mother House for her. She folded the document, placed it in the envelope, and gave it to me to take to the superior. I did as I was told and returned to the convent with a determination to help. I knew the community was in financial straits and that was enough for me to want to help.

I was teaching high school classes at the time and had loads of examination papers to correct. Many nights, after writing the grade marks on the papers, I would dream numbers when I slept. I didn't think them significant until one particular set kept recurring. Then I got an idea. Around that time there was to be the drawing of a million dollar lottery to mark the country's anniversary of independence. I decided that I would look for and buy a ticket with the numbers of my dream. My father and my brother-in-law had their own company and my dad drove the delivery truck to every part of the country. I wrote down the number and asked him to look for it. He was the only person I trusted to tell this number to.

One Saturday morning I was asked to go into an office in the city to pay a bill for Sister Emma. After paying the bill, I left the office with change of a twenty-dollar bill. I flew out of the door with such haste I bumped right into this little old man selling lottery tickets on the sidewalk. I apologized, helped him gather up the tickets that were scattered, then asked him to allow me to look through them to find a special number. I could not find the exact number I sought but there was one close enough so I bought as many tickets as the twenty dollars change could purchase. I thanked the vendor and sped off. When I got to the convent I went straight to the chapel. On a table on the side of the altar stood a statue of Mary as big as I was, as well as a smaller one of the Infant Jesus which I could lift. I took the tickets out of my pocket and placed them under the Infant Jesus, fervently said a prayer, and left.

The lottery was drawn that Saturday night, but the results would not be published in the newspaper until the following Monday which happened to be my birthday. That day I must have broken every rule in the convent. A nun's day is rigidly structured so that she does not do frivolous things like reading the newspaper in the middle of the morning. As soon as I heard the delivery man come to the front door I ran out and grabbed the newspaper from him before the receptionist or any of the other sisters took it, and hid it away until recreation time in the evening. I headed straight to the chapel, turned to the page with the lottery results, retrieved the tickets from their safe haven and compared the numbers. I could not believe my eyes! There in black and white was the identical number as the one on the four tickets in my hand!

I ran to Sister Emma's office jabbering excitedly and almost incoherently, laughing and crying simultaneously (sisters do not run but walk in a dignified manner, nor do they raise their voices or show emotions so openly). I told Sister Emma to sit down so she wouldn't get a heart attack from the shock. Then I showed her the paper and the tickets which I clutched tightly in my hand. She gave me a quizzical look when she saw the tickets and I knew I would have to explain how I had come by them, but that and any reprimand from her would just have to wait.

We telephoned the lottery office and sister asked the clerk: "Could there be any mistake in the number printed?" "No ma'am," the clerk assured her. We were told to go to the office with the tickets so that we could receive the check for the twenty thousand dollars they had brought us. The check went directly to the bank to pay that frightful bill that had caused so much distress. I didn't tell a soul; I was just so happy that I was able to help such a desperate situation; but Sister Emma insisted on telling everyone the story.

I soon became a firm believer in and advocate of "redemptive suffering" (a theory based upon Jesus' suffering and dying to redeem humankind). I did not romanticize about suffering but as I endeavored to mirror the gospels I reflected deeply on Jesus' ideal of "emptying oneself so that God can fill one," which did indeed entail enormous suffering. I had endured my share of physical agony. I suffered constant excruciating pains in my stomach, couldn't keep food down, and was therefore thin as a rake. Doctors thought I might have cancer of the stomach.

I spent two weeks in the hospital undergoing tests upon tests, refusing to be operated on, but continuing to pray for healing. I was given doses of herbal medicine which seemed somehow to take care of whatever was in my stomach. I also suffered terrible mental anguish. Besides the bouts of spiritual dryness, there was this constant fight to observe "blind" obedience. It was very difficult for me to do something I saw no sense or reason in but had to do because "the superior said to do it." I nevertheless swallowed my anger and resentment and spent long periods instead in silent prayer, even though I felt God was not listening to me.

One great lesson I had learned very early in religious life was that suffering was an unavoidable part of life over which we had no choice but we could choose the way we faced that suffering in whatever form it came. We could choose to endure the suffering with resentment and bitterness and become a sourpuss or we could accept our fate and make every effort to live our lives around the suffering finding meaning and even happiness where we can.

I tried to emulate Sister Emma who was always doing something for somebody else and thus neglecting herself. It soon became evident to me that while some people were genuinely appreciative of goodness done to or for them, others live just to take advantage of the kindness of others. I therefore became very cautious and selective of the people whom I helped. Thus armed with a certain detachment from everything and everyone around me, and the spiritual teachings of some of the famous saints of the church, particularly St Therese and St Francis, I felt strong enough to face any challenge.

When I was told that I was one of the sisters chosen to pioneer the mission to Liberia, I was humanly nervous but I also felt ready and prepared. Sister Emma, my friend and mentor, was one of the first sisters to know about the mission there and even volunteered to go but was declined because of her failing health. When she learned that I was going, she poured all her energies into gathering material for me to take. Unfortunately, she passed away two months before the mission was opened.

CHAPTER FOUR

Papers had to be processed and loose ends tied up before we could depart from Trinidad for the new mission to Liberia. Despite my being a very strict disciplinarian, my students were devastated when I told them I was going so far away. I had always tried to remain aloof so that I wouldn't grow close to anyone, yet many people were distraught over my departure. They continually asked, "Why you?" and I defiantly responded, "Why not me?" My most difficult task was saying good-bye to my family-my parents, my brothers, and sisters, and my three precious nieces, Tenille, Amanda, and Cassandra who meant the world to me.

While I remained unaffected as I said good-bye to students, friends, and sisters of the communities, saying good-bye to my family broke me up. I could not bear to witness their pain, and just for a moment I examined myself and wondered if I was being crazy to leave my home, my family and go to such a far away land. Tenille helped ease the tension by tearfully demanding: "Why do they have to send you, Auntie; why couldn't they send one of those grumpy old nuns?"

One week before our departure, three of the four of us chosen to go to Liberia, Sister Angela, an experienced missionary and nurse from South America, Sister Doris, an American teacher who had migrated to and lived in the Caribbean before she became a sister, and I, attended a special Mass at the Mother House in our honor. The fourth sister, Sister Monica, was teaching in a government school in one of the islands and could not leave before her contract was up, so she would be joining us later on. As we knelt before the altar, Father Benedict, a monk, spread his hands over our heads and prayed: "Go, ... and make disciples..."

We were venturing out into a land that was over six thousand miles away from "home," but for a missionary, "home" was wherever God sent him or her to work. So we were going in faith, the faith that had been nurtured, strengthened, tried, and tested, stretched over its limit but never broken during our years in the convent. We were specially chosen for this mission and, although given the choice to decline, we accepted the challenge, each confident in fulfilling the trust placed in her to be a pioneer, to be a real missionary. I was by far the youngest of the three sisters and, although firm in my beliefs and decisions, I was broad-minded, open to new ideas and discoveries.

We left Trinidad at the end of October 1989 and arrived in England where we spent a week to have medical shots and obtain visas to enter Liberia. We also replenished our supply of the all-important chloroquin, malaria medicine that we had begun taking two weeks before we left Trinidad. The superior in England had booked our flights to Liberia, and no one bothered to double check what kind of flight. It turned out that we were booked on a special, cheap, economy flight, which meant that we could not take the tons of stuff we had with us. The flight only allowed us twenty kilos of luggage whereas we each had two suitcases, all packed solid.

To take all of this with us would cost almost three thousand dollars, money which we definitely did not have. Sister Doris went to the counter and pleaded with the clerk: "But we are poor missionaries and we don't have that kind of money," to which the stone-faced woman heartlessly replied: "So what?" So, we chose one piece of luggage and left the rest with the sisters to send later on by more economical means. We soon boarded the plane for our journey to Liberia. The flight seemed endless, and every time we dozed off, we were awakened to partake of food or drink. After two stopovers we finally reached our destination.

We arrived at Roberts' International Airport in the middle of the night. This airport is situated in an area called Robertsfield, which is about forty miles from the capital, Monrovia. We were warmly greeted by Sister Ivy, the superior of the order of sisters we were replacing, Sister Marcia, a Pakistani sister of the same order and Sister Laura, a Liberian sister who was our driver and who was taking us to her community where we would stay until we got to our mission. As we drove through the streets we noticed much revelry and celebration, and when we asked what was happening we were reminded that it was the first Thursday of November, the day Liberians celebrate Thanksgiving Day. As we drove on Sister Ivy remarked that it might be the last time it would be celebrated for a long time. We had no idea why, but we were too tired to ask.

After what seemed like an endless journey, we arrived at the convent where we were to stay for just a while. Here we met Sister Bernadette, an American sister who was very warm and possessed a great sense of humor. Then there was Sister Mary Elizabeth, a Brazilian and the superior of the community. She had a "take charge" attitude and did indeed take charge of the situation. The third sister of the community was Sister Laura who didn't speak much and kept pretty much to herself. We thanked her for her immense kindness in getting us from the airport to the convent and we didn't see much of her again. Sister Elizabeth fussed to make sure we had a warm meal and everything we needed to be as comfortable as possible.

The next day I woke bright and early and walked around exploring. I could not believe my eyes. This convent was like any of the convents I had seen in America or England. It had modern furnishings with every imaginable utility and equipment. There was an electric stove, washer and dryer, television and VCR, stereo, all the modern electric kitchen gadgets, and innumerable books everywhere. While I was not big on luxury I did like fine things, and I could not help but hope that the convent we were going to live in was furnished like this one. When the other sisters awoke, they informed us that they had planned a beach picnic because the day after Thanksgiving was a school holiday and they were all school sisters. Before taking us to the beach, Sister Elizabeth gave us a grand tour of the city of Monrovia.

Sisters Angela, Doris, and I were impressed to see large, magnificent buildings such as the university, the Executive Mansion (where the president of the country resided with his entourage and cohorts), the Ducor Palace (the country's first five-star hotel), the Pan African Building, which housed several government and diplomatic offices, and other newly erected constructions. Ironically, the next street brought us right into the middle of the worst slum area I had ever seen. Here we saw stark poverty, evident signs of neglect and disrepair, as we passed various government and private buildings in different stages of dilapidation. The shopping area brought even more surprises.

The shopkeepers were mainly Lebanese and Indian businessmen, and the shops were packed with every conceivable item. I was awestruck by the large area that housed an open air market. I was told that one never paid the price a vendor requested but one "haggled" instead. Haggling was new to me because I was familiar with paying whatever the price was. When we finally got to the beach, we enjoyed the grand picnic planned by the sisters to welcome us to Liberia and the beginning of our missionary life.

We were delayed in Monrovia for a few days because of the long holiday weekend. Our only means of getting to Greenville City, the place of our mission, was by private airplane. And, the only service available was run by a Lebanese businessman who operated out of the city's second airport, Spriggs Payne Airfield. He had a fleet of small aircrafts which served the thirteen counties of the country. These aircrafts seated from two to seven persons but were very often loaded up with other cargo, including livestock and food supplies. Very often, businessmen from the other counties who came to the city to replenish their stocks would pay huge sums of money in bribes to hire the planes for their private use, which left other travelers stranded.

Since we were to be working in the southeast region of the country we were under a different bishop than the one in Monrovia. Bishop Henry had journeyed to Monrovia to welcome us, the newest members of his diocese, and would be traveling with us to our new home. Sister Jane, our general superior and the one who had accepted the invitation of Bishop Henry, had come with us, and Sister Ivy, the superior of the sisters we three were replacing, made up a traveling party of six. Therefore we needed to hire an entire airplane.

The only way we could procure one was for the bishop to do what everybody else did - he bribed the owner. I was disgusted when I learned this, but I said nothing to avoid embarrassing anyone. After obtaining the necessary papers we were on our way to our new home. Our pilot was one of the two foreign pilots who flew for this air service. He spoke very little English but managed to inform us that he had just moved out there from Spain because his wife had recently died leaving him with a three-year-old daughter. He and his daughter moved to Monrovia and sometimes he took her on flights with him because he hoped she would develop a love for flying and become a pilot like him. Two days after he took us safely to our destination, he perished when his plane developed engine trouble and plunged into the sea.

We arrived at the airfield of Greenville City and were greeted by brilliant sunshine, a cool sea breeze, two Ghanaian priests, Father Kwesi and Father Kofi, and two foreign sisters, Sister Fran, a German sister and Sister Rosa, a Brazilian, as well as a host of people all curious and anxious to meet the new mission sisters. As I reached across the luggage trolley to retrieve my suitcase, I felt a chill pass through my body and Sister Emma came to my mind. I caught a whiff of the Lily of the Valley cologne she loved and always bathed her face in and I spun around expecting to see her standing right behind me, but of course she wasn't there, she was dead.

Suddenly I realized how much I missed her and that I hadn't really mourned her passing. When she died I somehow did not take it seriously and felt as if she had gone away on one of the numerous trips she was always taking, so she would return soon enough. At that moment I felt extremely alone and scared, but as was my style, I pushed those negative feelings back, assumed a brave front, and moved on to greet everyone. I had stepped outside of the realm of the sheltered life I had known all my life and I had to be brave and strong in order to survive.

As Father Kwesi placed our three bags in the car, he gave Sister Jane a quizzical look and asked her if we had only come to visit for a while. Sister laughed and gave him the story about our luggage. Father Kofi seated Sister Fran and Sister Rosa, neither of whom drove as well as Sister Doris and I into the gray station wagon which belonged to the sisters but which he had driven, while Father Kwesi took the bishop and the other three sisters in his car, a white Ford Corolla for the short journey to the convent which we were told was only about two miles away.

We drove on a dirt road for about ten minutes then turned up into a driveway that seemed to stretch ahead for almost a mile. At the entrance of the driveway we saw two concrete buildings, newly painted in white with green bases and roofs. Father declared that this was the clinic. He did not stop for us to examine anything but made a sharp turn and there, up ahead, nestled among a profusion of palm and other fruit trees, was a stately building, also newly painted in white with green base and roof. There was a quaint round hut at the side that caught my fancy. Here before us lay our convent. The hut at the side built in the style of the local "palavar hut" was the chapel. What seemed like ten acres of land lay all around, but every inch was filled with some kind of tree. This was to be "home" for at least the next five years, the duration of our work contract.

The priests dropped us off but promised to be back to have lunch with us. As we disembarked and entered the house, I felt overawed. The interior was absolutely charming. The order of sisters we were replacing had been working in Liberia for over twenty years but because their members were dwindling they had to recall the communities serving there. They had built that convent, and one of the sisters had single-handedly collected funds and built the high school I would be working in. The sisters had furnished the house modestly but adequately. As one entered the front door there was a small sitting room on the left and just off to the right there was a large dining room which led into a sitting room. Just off that sitting room was a door that led out to an enclosed porch furnished with locally made chairs and tables and a large grass woven mat. Another door from the porch opened out to a corridor that led to the palavar hut. When this was opened up, we saw a tiny church that seemed as if it hadn't been used in months.

Back inside we went to inspect the sleeping area. There were five comfortable-sized bedrooms on one side of the house and two extra-large ones on the other. We realized immediately that these two large rooms were guest rooms because there were several beds in each of them. There were big, airy closets every-where, and a large storage room with lots of knicks and knacks. As we left that area we walked over to the other side of the house where we came into the kitchen. There was an electric stove, a large refrigerator, and all the modern kitchen gadgets and dishes to make our chores as easy and comfortable as possible, or so we hoped. A large laundry room was across from the kitchen, but beyond the kitchen was another room with two large concrete sinks and a high brick table on which sat two coal pots.

Sister Ivy must have seen the look of bewilderment and dis-belief on my face and quickly set about to explain the coal pots. Electricity in regions outside of Monrovia was intermittent, and since the stove was an electric one, coal was the alternative. I also noticed a quaint earthen water cooler and Sister Fran explained that we were never to drink water from the tap or well or anywhere except from that cooler. There was a whole ritual to follow in order to purify our drinking water which she said would be explained later. Since there was no electricity that day, Sisters Ivy, Fran, and Rosa told us to go and choose our bedrooms and unpack while they prepared a meal for us. We offered to help but they assured us that we would soon get our turns on the coal pots.

In about an hour the priests returned, and Sister Ivy called us to the large dining room which was laid out with the finest batik tablecloth and napkins and real china dishes. The sisters had prepared a delicious meal of rice, vegetables, and beef stew. As we heartily consumed this, our first meal in our new home we chatted and became acquainted with each other.

Sisters Ivy, Fran, and Rosa had all worked in Brazil before being assigned to Liberia. When they first began their mission there they had over fifty sisters spread out in communities in different parts of the country. Now, because the sisters had grown too old or sick or were required in other more urgent missions, they had only about ten left. Sisters Fran and Rosa had completed their contracts and remained only until we arrived to replace them. Though they spoke very halting English, they were warm and welcoming. They were very sad to be leaving but felt that they had done their share in promoting God's work in that country.

The two priests, Father Kwesi and Kofi, were completely opposite in every way. Father Kwesi was over six feet tall and was large in stature, while Father Kofi was short and slim. While Father Kwesi chatted exuberantly and ate heartily, Father Kofi was very quiet and hardly ate at all. Father Kwesi told us that when the diocese had experienced a lack of priests, the bishop had asked the bishop of his diocese in Ghana to send a few priests because there was an influx of priestly vocations in Ghana.

That's how he came to be in Liberia. When the church was built in Greenville City, which was in Sinoe County, he was sent there. He was not happy because this area was very desolate and difficult, so none of the priests wanted to be sent there. He came nevertheless, but after two years the loneliness was too much for him. There was, besides, the need for new outstations in nearby towns so he asked his bishop to send him an assistant. Father Kofi, a priest of only one year, was sent.

When every last morsel of the meal was eaten and the dishes cleared away and washed we were advised to take a rest. The priests told Sister Ivy to bring us to the mission house where they lived about three o'clock, after their siesta, so they could show us around. Then they bade us farewell and left. I had intended to choose the last bedroom, but Sister Jane chose it first, so until she left us I slept in the first room. Sisters Angela and Doris chose the second and third rooms, while Sisters Ivy, Fran, and Rosa decided to use one of the guest rooms. While the others rested briefly, I opened the back door and explored the grounds until it was time to visit with the priests.

Sister Rosa was the designated driver for the grand tour of Greenville City. The convent was situated in an area called Farmersville which had once been a cemetery. It was about one mile off the main road and very sandy because the ocean was quite close. When we got to a paved road, we drove for another ten minutes, then turned unto another unpaved road. Sister explained that the church and priests' house were along this road, but it also led to the port area where they were going to take us first. Soon we could feel the sea breeze, and I grew excited to learn that the sea was so close. I love the ocean and looked forward to exploring the beautiful little coves Sister Rosa pointed out as we drove along.

I remarked on the very modern houses we passed, and Sister Fran explained that these were for employees of the port. We were informed that the manager of the port was from the Caribbean and I was curious to make his acquaintance. I didn't have to wait long. Parked along the road was a most elegant, expensive car, and as we drove by a man disembarked and stopped our car. He opened the car doors and invited us out, boldly inquiring who we were and where we were from. I thought that was rather rude, and when it was my turn I remained silent for a while and responded only when Sister Doris nudged me.

Stanley announced that he was from the same country as Sister Angela but had worked many years in my home country. Sister Angela asked him how he came to be working in Liberia, but he ignored her question. Instead he launched into an accolade of his accomplishments, giving himself several pats on the back. I disliked him immediately, especially since I felt extremely uncomfortable under his lecherous stare. He was far from bashful and extremely talkative. Sister Jane cut him short tactfully by announcing that we had an appointment with the priests and didn't want to be late. He paused, then invited us to come by whenever we wanted.

Our next stop was the shopping area and large open-air market. Sister Doris and I were amazed to see that the shops carried all the items we were familiar with and would need. Most of the shopkeepers were Lebanese, and when I remarked to one of them that I was surprised to see Lebanese here, he replied: "Missy, if you go to the moon you will find my people living there." Some of the other businessmen were "Fulah." Sister Ivy explained that this was a tribe of people who had come from Guinea. The local businessmen and women preferred the open-air market to ply their goods, which were mainly vegetables and fresh fish. Greenville City consisted mainly of the Kru and Saapo tribes who were farmers as well as a large Fanti community which came from Ghana. They lived along the oceanfront and fishing was their mainstay.

As we continued our journey to the mission I noticed two gas stations, several beer gardens and the main hospital along the main road. The streets of the city area were all well paved and Sister Fran informed us that a German community had lived here many years ago and had undertaken that project. She said that they had also built the hospital which had been well stocked and well kept but had fallen into disrepair after the Germans left.

I was fascinated to learn that within Sinoe County there were five logging companies. Not for one moment did I think that I would have needed to know this bit of information or would be dealing in close proximity with them during my stay in Liberia. As we drove through the streets of the town I compared the types of houses and their sizes. There were wooden shacks, three- storied brick structures, and huge zinc constructions. Sister Ivy explained that the natives strove to erect concrete houses which indicated their elevated status. Foreigners, on the other hand, recognizing the beauty and value of the different trees of the timber forest, utilized the timber to build themselves elaborate homes and furnishings.

After our brief but informative tour of the town, we were taken to the Catholic mission. As we drove into the gateway, we observed the quaint, little structure that was our house of worship. Right behind that was the Senior High School, then along that side was the priests' houses. All of these buildings were along the bank of a river. On the right side of the compound was the Junior High School. A sizable playing field completing the U-shaped area.

I fell in love with the place but could not help feeling depressed to see everything looking so unkempt, neglected, and gloomy. I was confident, however, that this feeling of doom and gloom was not going to last for long. I knew Sister Doris and I were going to roll up our sleeves and work our fingers to the bone to improve everything, so great was our energy and fervor to make this mission succeed. The motto of the order to which we belonged was: "With zeal I am zealous..." and this was a perfect example to live out that motto.

I did not romanticize about such things but I knew I had received many graces from God, especially since making my perpetual vows. I was well aware of the moments when God was present to me in many ways and I also experienced severe "desert" periods when no matter how hard I screamed or gently whispered his name, he was nowhere near, or so I thought. I had come to believe firmly that a life rooted in God was a life filled with humility and openness to his Spirit. It was a life where the Holy Spirit did the leading, a state of surrender where we found ourselves drawn to a place we never would have freely chosen.

Jesus asks us to act upon his words to "love one another," and this we can do because, with God's help, everything is possible. The challenge is getting ourselves in the frame of mind where we can truly enter into his life and trust in his strength. I was determined to draw deeply from this strength and the numerous graces I felt I had been blessed with. I would certainly need all the help I could get--spiritual and other-- in a place like this if I was going to be effective in any way in doing the work that I was sent to do.

The priests were waiting for us, and first they gave us a tour of their house. Father Kwesi lived in the main house which sat atop a small hill overlooking the river. The view was breathtaking and I couldn't help wishing aloud that the convent had been built here instead. Father immediately responded that the sisters always said the same thing. It was just sad to see the yard overgrown with tall weeds, broken windows hanging by their hinges, torn mosquito screens, tattered curtains, dust and cobwebs everywhere. Father Kofi lived in an annex built unto the main house and that was in an even worse state of disrepair. The order of sisters to which I belonged cared for the poor and outcast, the aged and helpless, but we cared in a special way for our priests once they allowed us. I knew therefore that these houses were not going to remain in such a dilapidated state for long.

Father Kwesi took Sister Angela, Doris, and me to see the school buildings while the other sisters stayed and chatted with the group of parishioners who had gathered in the father's house. We first went to the Senior High School. This consisted of three large classrooms and an office area which was divided into one large room and two smaller ones. There was no ceiling, so the zinc roof and planks were exposed; nor was the floor finished. I sensed that the building was hastily constructed, and I asked

Father if this was so.

He explained that there were two American sisters who were teaching in the junior school. They always had lots of money which they distributed freely to students and their families. There was no high school so Father Kwesi suggested they help erect one. On their visit home one year, one of the sisters, Paula, collected funds from all her communities and returned to Greenville to build the most needed high school. However, it had to be hastily built because her contract was up at the end of the year, the year before we went there. There was lots of work to be done here.

We walked across the courtyard and entered the junior school. There were two rooms, one of which was the principal's office and the other the teachers' lounge. A door off the wall of the principal's office led to a dark, dank, gloomy room which served as a book room. Back out on the corridor we viewed classrooms on either side which housed Grades Nine down to Kindergarten. There was a large hall at the end of the corridor and this was supposed to be an auditorium but was in severe disrepair. Parts of the roof were torn off, broken windows were hanging, and it appeared to be a storage space for broken desks and benches.

All the classrooms were dark, hot, and airless, contained no pictures or posters, furnished with heavy wooden benches and the walls were painted in a dark brown color. Father explained that some of the grades held as many as sixty students. He continued chatting nervously and we could see it was to hide his embarrassment at the gloomy scene that faced us. As we made our way across the courtyard to rejoin the other sisters he asked Sister D and me if we had any questions, but our minds were reeling with plans to make those rooms into classrooms we were accustomed to working in.

The first Sunday after our arrival, Bishop Henry came to celebrate Mass to welcome us to his diocese. He resided in Harper, which was part of Maryland County situated at the southernmost tip of Liberia. Only a river separated that area from the Ivory Coast. This town was about forty-five miles from Greenville and he was driven by his assigned driver, Bayley. Normally this journey should have taken two or three hours but it sometimes took a whole day depending on the condition of the vehicle. None of the interior roads of the country is paved and in the dry season red dust blows everywhere, whereas when the rains came, there was knee-deep mud.

Bishop Henry brought some of the missionaries who served in his parish and they stayed in the convent with us. There was Sister Lynn who had lived and worked in Greenville before. She had a knack for rubbing people the wrong way so we soon learned that when she was around we had to dish out extra large servings of charity. Then there were two lay missionaries who served in the bishop's parish. One was Carol, who was from the Caribbean. She fondly attributed our presence in Liberia to her recommendation of our order to the bishop. I was happy to meet her because I had known her cousin, Greg, when I was studying in the seminary. Before he could complete his studies, however, he had succumbed to a serious illness and passed away. Carol had a powerful personality which made her stand out in many ways and even slightly feared by others. The other lay missionary was Beth, who was down-to-earth, funny, friendly and at-home wherever she went.

At Mass that Sunday morning the tiny church was packed to overflowing. Some members who had not attended Church for the entire year turned out to welcome us and to pay respect to the bishop who was revered in all his parishes. Because Greenville was so far and remote, his visits there were rare. The women were dressed in their best "lappa" suits. These suits were made out of at least six yards of colorful African cotton prints.

There was a jacket style top and a straight regular skirt over which a special piece was tied in a unique way. This extra piece was called the 'lappa' and served many purposes. The women would use this "lappa" to strap a baby to their back, as a blanket if nighttime caught them traveling, as a towel, tablecloth, and a head-tie. The elderly men were dressed in two, and three-pieced suits which they wore very proudly. The younger men and women preferred Western-styled clothes. I was taken aback at the chaos that reigned as the people filled the church. They all greeted each other at the top of their voices. Everyone spoke as if they were on the streets or in the fields, but the moment the bishop and his entourage entered the sanctuary you could hear a pin drop. From the way everyone sang lustily and offered their prayers sincerely and honestly, I knew this was an extraordinary community.

After the Mass, which lasted almost two hours, there was a large, open-air party in the school yard. This party was hosted by a very elite group in the parish who called themselves the Knights and Ladies of Marshall. The Grand Master of this group was also the president of the parish council, while the other members were elders and leaders in the church and prominent members of the larger community.

When it came to making long-winded speeches, the Liberians outshone everyone else I had encountered. At that gathering in our honor, every leader and almost every member of the parish gave a speech. While their words were warm, sincere, and welcoming, many of them were bold enough to suggest that we follow the example set by the sisters before us who gave money and material objects freely.

I was infuriated to hear this, because I didn't want to believe that the members of this community had become lazy and dependent on free handouts. Of course I intended to help needy students and their parents but my method was going to be different. Believing in upholding the dignity of the poor, when anyone in my care needed either money to pay a bill or something material, I always made them perform some small task so they would feel that they had earned what they needed. I intended to use the same method here. After all, there was enough grass to be cut, yard to be swept, and walls to be painted.

After the speeches, the parish council president presented us with a large wooden key of the city and then invited us to partake of the feast that was laid before us. We were introduced to all the renown and favorite Liberian dishes. There was palm butter which looked like curry. It was made from the palm nuts that grew on tall trees around the campus yard which was seasoned with a lot of hot pepper, fish (dry and fresh), crawfish, chicken, and every other different kind of meat available. This was served with rice. Then there was "foo foo," made from boiled, pounded cassava, and this was served with hot pepper soup. There was a variety of "greens," palavar sauce, potato greens, cassava leaves, all cooked to perfection in the special "red" oil and served with rice.

We were then introduced to "palm wine," one of the delicacies attributed to the more skillful men. A palm tree was felled, fire was applied to the section that contained the "heart" and a white, frothy, and most intoxicating juice was extracted. Only the most astute and skilled could draw the sweetest and most delectable juice. This juice was consumed in gallons by men, women, and children. There was a myth that the thicker and sweeter it was, the stronger and more intoxicating it was. Liberians love a celebration and approach an occasion to celebrate with much pomp and ceremony. That day we witnessed them in all their splendor and, after graciously accepting the warm welcome, we left the remnants of the party and returned to the convent.

When we arrived at the convent and I entered my room, I saw immediately that something was wrong. Some of the glass louvers had been removed and some were broken. There were mosquito screens on every window as well as iron bars on the inside. The screens on my windows were slit and a big hole torn in one of them. Through this hole a long stick had been pushed and an attempt had been made to reach the few things I had laid out on my table. I was shocked and enraged as I surveyed this scene and I reacted by screaming: "We've been robbed, check your rooms, we've been robbed!" The other sisters had remained in the sitting room but when they heard me they came running and went to check their rooms.

When everyone found their rooms untouched they hurried into my room to investigate further. My bath towel had been pulled through the hole and stolen, and a bag with my family pictures had been taken and scattered on the ground outside the window. This made me even more mad as I felt my privacy intruded upon. My spirits were dampened and I remained angry and depressed for the rest of the day, wanting to seek out the culprits and punish them.

The next day the bishop came to the convent to give us our specific orders before returning to his home. He informed me that Father Kwesi had assumed the role of principal of the Senior High School but quickly pointed out that Father's first responsibility was to be the shepherd to the people of the parish. I was therefore to be the new principal. He then jested that when he informed the members of the parish council at the meeting they held after the party the day before, some of them scoffed, remarking that I was "too young!" Sister Doris was to assume responsibility of the junior school from Father Kofi until Sister Monica arrived. Sister Doris opted to teach instead of being an administrator, so she was eager for Sister Monica to get there and assume her responsibilities.

Sister Doris and I wanted to plunge headlong into transforming the interiors and exteriors of the schools, but we had to be a little patient because we had to return to Monrovia to attend an orientation seminar for all new missionaries. Somehow it didn't seem right that we had to leave for two weeks just as we had arrived, especially when there was so much work to be done. Sister Angela was required to attend nursing sessions in Harper before attending that seminar so she had gone ahead with the bishop to Harper and would then fly to Monrovia.

Not wanting to be disobedient or to appear unsociable, we locked up the house, gave the keys to Father Kwesi, who said he would stay there so that no one would try to break in, and then we boarded a flight to Monrovia. The seminar was going to be held in the diocese of Gbarnga, which was a two-hour drive from the city of Monrovia. When we got to Monrovia we headed for the convent where we had first stayed and where we were supposed to meet Sister Angela. We got there two hours early, so Sister Doris and I headed straight for the shops downtown.

We took a taxi which charged us forty cents each and went first to the Waterside area, which comprised the open air markets. Every conceivable item could be purchased at dirt cheap prices in these markets. Sister Doris had made up her mind about teaching the kindergarten class and had formulated her plans to transform the classroom. The first item she bought was two gallons of the brightest yellow paint and enough paint brushes for a few volunteers to assist her.

During Mass that Sunday in Greenville I had been appalled at the starkness of the church. There were no flower vases, the altar linens were in tatters, and the altar brass could use a good cleaning. I had been competently trained by Sister Clare to care for a church sanctuary and I had amassed a lot of experience and practice as I served as sacristan in every parish I had worked in. I loved caring for the altar sanctuary and the church, and I was determined to do the same for the church in Greenville. The parish was dedicated to St. Joseph, the Worker. I was most certainly going to enlist his assistance in making his church beautiful.

Since Christmas was less than a month away I bought cloth and gold trimmings to make new altar covers, and linens for Mass. I bought flower vases to place the arrangements I would create to decorate the altar, then I secretly bought Christmas gifts for the two priests and the two sisters. By the time Sister Doris and I finished our shopping we were exhausted but very pleased. We returned to the convent where we hoped Sister Angela would be so we could travel to Gbarnga.

When Sister Doris and I arrived at the convent we were

greeted by Sister Annette, a sister we hadn't met before. She was the cousin of Sister Laura, but she resided and worked in Harper. She told us that she was the Youth Coordinator for the diocese and I could see why. Sister Annette was very attractive (her father was a foreigner and her mother Liberian), friendly, full of life, and ever so kind. Just from looking at her and hearing her speak, I could imagine young people flocking to her. When she heard that we were going to take a taxi to Gbarnga she would not hear of it. She immediately summoned her driver to bring around her jeep and offered to take us to our destination. We were most grateful and made full use of the air-conditioned, four-wheel drive vehicle and thoroughly enjoyed the journey.

When we arrived at the mission in Gbarnga we were greeted by Bishop Dotu as well as close to one hundred missionaries who had come to work in this tiny, seemingly insignificant country. This mission gave the appearance of a very prosperous one. The bishop's house was luxurious and we could see that he lived a lavish lifestyle. The whole compound was well cared for. I observed a large, elaborate building in the background and when I asked what that was, I was told that it was the seminary where young men came to study for the priesthood.

We were introduced to Peace Corps workers, lay missionaries, and religious brothers, sisters and priests from various parts of the world. There were two groups of sisters from different orders in India. While everyone else appeared shy or reserved, these nuns were rather extrovert, over-friendly, and somewhat pushy and bossy, but no one really paid any attention to them.

We were taken to rooms in the boarding house, but as we followed the young man who led the way I got a sudden dose of the creeps. As I joined Sister Doris and headed to the hall for the first session, I voiced this fear to her. She immediately confessed that she felt every bit as uneasy as I did, so we devised a plan. We would stay the night, but then I would suddenly get very "ill" and have to return home.

The first session that evening was given by Archbishop

Mike, the archbishop of Monrovia. We were told that he was very outspoken and firmly protected his faith and his church from anyone or anything that wanted to bring them harm. I don't remember much of what he said but quite clearly I remember his opening remarks: "Take off your shoes, you're on holy grounds!" his loud voice boomed in the silence of the night.

He justified his statement by speaking of missionaries who enter strange lands and proceed to push their teachings down the throats of the people who were ignorant and resisted. One lecturer, whose classes I had attended when I was studying at the seminary back home, had taught us the same thing, so I understood what Archbishop Mike was saying. He warned us not to take this approach in our missions. He advised us to take the people at whatever stage they were in life and work with them from there, not above their heads.

As the evening wore on, my discomfort grew. I made my way out of the hall to go back to my room, and as I grew closer I saw someone at the door trying to get in. I cleared my throat loudly and the person ran off, but that did it for me. I was not staying another night much more two weeks in that place. I hurried back to the hall and found Sister D. I told her what had just happened, and we decided right away to seek out Bishop Dotu. We were directed to his house where we found him drinking cold beer in his air-conditioned house.

After exchanging greetings we came right to the point gently brushing aside his attempt to socialize with us. Sister explained that I was in a lot of pain and needed to return to Greenville. He offered to have me checked out at the nearby well-equipped hospital, but I declined explaining that it was very personal and I would be okay once I got home and took the necessary precautions. He seemed puzzled, but nevertheless agreed to hire a taxi to take us directly to Greenville. We had to be up and at the front of his house at 5:00A.M. the next morning. We thanked him and went directly to sleep so that we would be up and ready at the crack of dawn.

At 5:00A.M. the next morning, Sister Doris and I boarded a yellow taxicab from Gbarnga, destination Greenville City, Sinoe.   Bishop Dotu informed us that the entire cab was chartered for us so we occupied the back seat, but as we drove off Sister D informed the driver that he could pick up a passenger in the vacant front seat to make a few extra dollars. He was elated and opportunely picked up his first passenger, a woman over two hundred pounds, laden with two heavy pieces of baggage. Her destination was Zwedru, the next large town about sixty miles from Gbarnga. The main street through the city of this town was paved so we had a smooth, uneventful ride for about ten miles then, as we hit the dirt road, our troubles began.

The crude tracks which drivers must use were cut out by the logging companies scattered throughout the country to take their logs from the forest or their plants to the nearest ports. Rough, unsteady bridges were constructed over rivers but very often travelers had to stop when they came to a bridge, climb out of their vehicles, search for missing planks or find substitutes, rebuild bridges, then continue their journey. The soil along these tracks was red sand. In the rainy season it turned to red mud but in the dry season, which was the time we were traveling, the dust is loose and covers everything and everyone in its path.

The sudden lurch unto the dirt track brought our vehicle to a sudden stop. When the driver attempted to revive the engine it refused to budge.   He didn't bat an eyelid but disembarked, removed a plank of wood from under his seat, opened the engine, and gave a few firm taps to the parts. When he returned and tried the engine again, it turned without hesitation. This man certainly seemed capable of coping with the adventures of traveling on these roads, and we were once more on our way.

It was a hot, humid day with the sun scorching down on us but that did not deter us from enjoying the beauty of the countryside and the different towns we passed through.   As we reached a town called Tappita, the car had a flat tire, so while the driver sought a shop to repair it we stretched our legs and looked around for decent facilities to use. There are no roadside inns or public bathrooms in these remote places, so travelers must learn to use the bush, and we were no exception. Luckily for us, there was a Lebanese shopkeeper and his wife who invited us in and offered us cold drinks, and we welcomed that opportunity to make use of their facilities. I was grateful for this hospitality because neither Sister D nor I was ready for the "bush treatment."

When the tire was repaired and we resumed our journey, we had another passenger. Luckily he was a skinny man, so he fit himself on the edge of the seat between the woman in the front seat and the driver. We drove for about an hour, and as we entered a town called Juarzon, there was a loud bang, then a heavy thud. I felt as it the bottom of the car had dropped off, but when the driver stopped to investigate, he discovered that the entire exhaust had broken off and was hanging by a piece of wire.

Very calmly and expertly the driver removed the broken exhaust pipe, opened the trunk and place it on top of our two bags. When we drove off once more the car sounded like a jet, which caused passersby to stare. A few miles on in the middle of nowhere, the driver was flagged down by a young boy carrying a tire on his head. He wanted to get to the nearest town to have the tire repaired and begged the driver to take him. The tire was placed in the trunk, the front door was opened, and the boy climbed in and sat on the woman's ample lap. As we ambled on the three passengers in the one front seat chatted merrily with the driver until we reached the town called Zwedru where all three passengers disembarked.

Zwedru was the hometown of President Davis. Looming in the background we could see the massive mansion being erected to commemorate his coming birthday. Amidst some scattered shabby shops and buildings, we saw this oasis of newly constructed buildings surrounded by lush green customized gardens. We were informed that this replica of a Manhattan cafe represented an ice-cream parlor and entertainment center being erected by the president's wife to leave her mark on the history of the town.

Tension seemed prevalent in this town and security was extra tight. There was a check point of soldiers as one entered and another as one left. These soldiers were supposed to check documents or vehicles, but once the driver or passengers of the vehicles passed the traditional dollars they were allowed to pass freely. Sometimes foreigners were harassed and even detained by the soldiers just so they could obtain as much money as they demanded. We did not experience any harassment, but the soldiers were extremely hostile so the driver added a few extra dollars and only then were we allowed to proceed in peace.

Very soon after that we arrived in Greenville City and went to the priests' house to collect the keys for our house. We did not realize it, but we were both covered from head to toe in red dust. When we arrived on the school campus some of the teachers who were gathered there ran out to the car. One of them who had a really big mouth and was completely tactless let out a cackle of laughter and exclaimed, "Yee, sista, now you look like a real African!" When we finally got home it took several buckets of water to wash away the dirt which had caked our eyelashes, and the inside of our nostrils. The taste of the dirt stayed in my lungs for days after.

CHAPTER FIVE

School was still in progress and there were a few more weeks before the Christmas break. The Senior High School was preparing for a very significant event in December of that year. The first grade twelve to be educated there was preparing for graduation, a landmark in the history of the school and the community. Before the Senior High School was built, when the students graduated from ninth grade they entered one of the three public senior high school from which they graduated after taking the national exams in twelfth grade.

The group of students preparing for graduation had done extremely well at the national exams. Everyone was surprised when a female student, Sue, received top grades in all the subjects. She beat her male counterparts Peter and James who were forerunners for the title of "Dux" of the class. As the "Dux" of the class, Sue automatically became the valedictorian, much to the envy of the male students. I didn't really know the students of this class, so when Father Kwesi requested that I train them for the ceremony, I used that opportunity to make their acquaintance.

The most outstanding student was James, a brilliant and exceptionally intelligent young man who was completely blind in one eye and partially blind in the other. The sisters before us had sought medical help for his condition without any success. Every time James was examined by the eye specialist and given medication, his parents forbade him to use it. Instead they peppered his eyes! "Peppered your eyes, James?" I asked in bewilderment. "Yes sister, we Africans believe that pepper drives away evil. So whatever part of the body is affected is peppered."

Then there was Sue. She belonged to a very prominent family in the town and everyone had high hopes that she would attend college and become someone important. She soon became my shadow, which made Father Kwesi teasingly declare, "Sister, I think Sue has a crush on you!" This annoyed me because she was indeed becoming a pest and even followed me to the convent when I left school in the evenings. I soon found out why I was the object of her affections.

Like many young people from these small towns who dreamed of bigger things, Sue was no different. As soon as they graduated from school they flocked to the city, Monrovia, to seek bigger things. They moved into homes of relatives who were already overburdened and almost poverty-stricken. In an effort to fulfill their big dreams, they sought "sponsors" from among the missionaries. Sue was unhappy about the untimely departure of the previous sisters who were so generous, because she had hoped that one of them would sponsor her through college. When we replaced the sisters who left, she soon transferred her plan onto me, but once she got to know me she would find out that it wasn't going to work. Every time she spoke to me and hinted that she wanted to go to college but didn't have the money, I pretended not to understand, and soon she lost interest in having me as her sponsor. It wasn't that I didn't want to help her or any of the others, but I found their demands unfair and selfish.

In that society, the education of girls is not important to parents. Instead, the families would spend hundreds of dollars in purchasing expensive clothes and accessories for the girls in the hope of catching a man. Polygamy was widely practiced in that country so no one really cared about getting married. Parents' main concern was that their daughters could find men to help pay the bills and run the household. It amazed me how they could find the money for such things but they couldn't find it for the children's education. I had gone there to help, but I was going to help in ways that made them better people, able to stand on their own two feet, not on mine or any of the other missionaries'.

The day of graduation was greeted with much pomp and splendor. Sister Brenda, the coordinator of the Catholic schools of the diocese, was invited and came for the occasion. She praised everyone for their excellent work and presented each graduate with a certificate which I had prepared on a brand new, battery-operated word processor I had found in Father Kwesi's office. He was delighted to see it being used because he had received it as a gift but, not knowing how to operate it, had simply chucked it in a corner in the office. Parents and relatives filled the church to capacity to witness this auspicious and memorable event in the lives of these students. After many speeches, tumultuous handshaking, hugging, and picture-taking, everyone wound their way to their homes where the celebration continued.

Christmas was one week away, and as we prepared to celebrate our first Christmas away from family or friends, we tried to distract ourselves from the threatening homesickness that hung like huge clouds over us. Sister Angela had to make a short trip to Harper for a few days, and school was closed until early February. That Sunday, while Sister D busied herself preparing a modest lunch, I climbed one of the mango trees in the yard and just bawled my eyes out.

I missed my family so much, especially my three nieces and my sister, Judy, who was more of a big sister to me than I was to her. She was very wise for her age and longed to break out, as I had, and be different. She and our brother, David, had been part of a weekend retreat for youths and eventually became members of the Church, much to the consternation of our mother. Judy sensed that she was called to a different life than that lived by my family and confided this to me. Even though I did not share such a close and open relationship with the others, I missed them just the same!

As I sat and reminisced, I wondered what they would be doing at that time. A few weeks earlier I had received a letter from my mother. She said Tenille and Mandy missed me dreadfully and asked constantly, "When is our 'fun' Aunty coming home?" With them I could be the kid I forgot to be when I was growing up. With them I could give freely of my love without fear of being rejected, I could enjoy the simple things kids love to do. I found my joy in making other people happy and I felt completely fulfilled when I saw how happy these kids were.

I loved taking them to the beaches, for long drives or walks in the country when we visited Marlene and Steve in their new home. I missed cuddling baby Sandy and seeing all the baby things she had begun doing (she was one month when I left home). I was suddenly brought out of my reverie by Sister D's crisp, sharp voice cautioning me that there could be snakes in that tree and reminding me that it was lunch time.

After sharing a simple meal of rice, corn, and tinned meat, sister suggested that we go and work on the church. I readily agreed, hoping to channel my energies into beautifying the church in preparation for Christmas instead of succumbing to homesickness or depression. Plunging myself into work or in doing something for someone in need whenever I felt depression creeping up always worked in pushing it aside, so I was going to apply that remedy now.

After a few hours of steady work, the interior of the church assumed a whole new look - new linens, new vases for the floral arrangements I would place in them, banners, and posters. The floor was mopped and polished not with any electric polisher but on our hands and knees. Father Kwesi had gone with Sister Angela to Harper, so while Sister D worked in the junior school, with Father Kofi's help, Father Kwesi's house was transformed.

I had secretly bought material and sewed curtains for the living room, curtains and a bedspread for the bedrooms, and tablecloths. I began sweeping and removing cobwebs, but soon the awestruck mission boys Robert and Samuel, began to help so we were finished in a short time. When every space had been thoroughly cleaned we put up the curtains and redecorated Father's room and the living room.

Father Kofi and the two boys stood and stared at me perplexed. They said they didn't know what to make of me. That was the first time they had seen one of the sisters with a broom in her hand. I ventured to ask what the other sisters had done, and I was told that they paid people to do everything for them, and apparently the dilapidated state of the church and priest's house didn't bother them in the least. I told them that I hated dirt and I loved to clean, so there wasn't going to be any dirt around while I was there.

Sister Angela and Father Kwesi returned two days before Christmas. Sister Doris had taken a dried branch from one of the trees in the garden and painted it white. When it was dried we placed it in an empty bucket in the living room and decorated it with trinkets we had discovered in the storeroom and with some we had made ourselves. We had each procured gifts for each sister and the two priests, and these we wrapped in gay, decorative paper and placed under the tree. We did our best to infuse a festive, Christmas feeling.

When Christmas day dawned, we joined the community at large for a beautiful celebration at church, then we invited the priests to dine with us for lunch. We distributed gifts and the fathers were ever so surprised to find so many wrapped packages for them under the tree. Father Kwesi then told us about returning to find a cleaned decorated house. He said he almost fainted and cried with joy because no one had ever done that for him before.

Having spent such a joyous day, we didn't pay much attention to the news, or rumors of war in the city, Monrovia, that were reported on the evening BBC news. Since rumors were rampant in these small towns and events were blown out of proportion, we felt that things were not as bad as were reported. How wrong we were!

The news reported that a certain Liberian, Ray Harper, who had been part of the Doe government and who had stolen money from the government and fled to the United States, had escaped from prison in the United States. He had sought refuge in Sierra Leone where he silently and connivingly amassed rebel troops and trained them for battle. Then on Christmas Eve day, he entered Monrovia and attacked the city with the intention of overthrowing the president, Samuel Doe. The force of this news did not hit us immediately because Monrovia was over one hundred miles from our town, so we felt safe for the time being.

Without trepidation or hesitation, Sister Angela gathered her staff and opened the clinic at the beginning of the new year while Sister Doris and I plunged headlong into preparing the schools for the new semester. When we got to the school campus, Sister D and I went our separate ways into our particular department. In the senior high I went first to the classrooms. Everything was covered in dust and cobwebs hung like lace curtains from the ceiling.

I wasted no time in cleaning. I removed my veil and scapular, rolled up my sleeves, and began by pulling down cobwebs, then sweeping. Then I got down on my knees and began to scrub the floors before I painted them. No matter what day of the week or time of day, once the school doors were opened students and even adults flocked there just to be in the presence of the priests and the sisters. When some of the students observed me doing "dirty" work, they stood and gaped. A few bold ones came up to me and offered to help, and soon I had a team of workers who made the work disappear in much less time than it would have taken me working alone.

By the end of the day everyone stood back and admired their achievement. When we had finished dusting, sweeping, scrubbing, and painting the three classrooms, we attacked the office area. Father Kwesi's office was the first room and I had plans for it once he left but he didn't seem eager to vacate it as yet. So I chose the small room at the back next to a large store room to be my office. That room had a single window that framed a terrific view of the river. The numerous cobwebs covering the stark, undecorated, unfurnished walls did not deter my determination to establish my office there.

The walls and floors were scrubbed and painted. The can of light blue paint I discovered in the store room soon found its way on the walls and the remnant of gray was spread carefully on the floor so that it adequately covered every inch of space. While that dried we proceeded to clean out the store room. There we found sacks of rice, bags of beans, cans of oil, and cartons of tinned meat, as well as various kinds of hardware. Seeing the foodstuff gave me an idea.

Father Kwesi was away from the mission during all our commotion and I was glad of this. Robert and Samuel, the mission boys, were among those helping to clean. They had access to the kitchen at the back of Father Kofi's house, so I quickly gave them enough stuff to prepare a meal for everyone who was working so rigorously. They were timid because they were terrified of Father Kwesi - everyone was except me. I told them that if he objected, I would take the blame, and that calmed their fears.

I knew that once physically fortified they would work even harder. Some of the young men got caught up in the spirit and energy of cleaning so zealously that they procured swipers, and before long all the grass around the school had been cut flat. Now it was my turn to stand back and marvel, and I was certainly effusive in my praises. The paint on the walls and floor in my office space soon dried, but I had no furniture. I hung the curtains I had sewed for the window and the door and sat on the floor taking mental notes of what was needed to make the room look like an office. For starters, I would need a desk and chair, and a bookshelf or two would be welcome. What I couldn't buy or obtain readymade I would improvise. I sat cross-legged hand under my chin and deep in thought as I was already planning the semester when Father Kwesi walked into the yard.

He could not believe the sight before his eyes. Young men and women too arrogant to offer assistance previously or too lazy to lift a finger, were singing loudly and dancing around joyously as they wielded brooms, swipers, rakes and whatever else they could use to clean their school campus. Perplexed, bewildered, and in utter disbelief, Father stomped over to where I was sitting on the floor and declared, "Sister-ya, what spell you put over my children-O?" I had noticed that the Liberians always added "ya" and "O" to their words and Father had quickly adapted this manner of speech. In mock cockiness, I saucily retorted, "Just my special brand of magic, Father."

As he helped me to my feet I took him to inspect the interior of the classrooms and the store room, then I casually mentioned that I had given the boys some foodstuff to prepare a meal for the students working so diligently. I waited for him to admonish me or make a scathing remark characteristic of him, but it never came. Father Kwesi looked at me tenderly and softly replied, "You are like a real mother, exactly what these children need-just don't spoil them." This confirmed my suspicions that under that stern, almost hostile appearance there lay a gentle, loving person.

We paused when we got to the door of his office. I had not wanted to intrude on his privacy, so I did not enter that room to clean it but I had made curtains and set aside paint for the walls and floor in case he wanted it redone. Well, indeed he did. When he saw the other rooms he pleaded, "Sister, you will fix my office like that too, ya?"

I promised to give it the same royal treatment but not before he guaranteed that the carpenter would make two bookshelves, one standing and one hung on the wall for my office. He had an extra desk and chair in his office, so with the help of two able-bodied students we transferred them to my room. As Father stood in his office and held the chair on which I had climbed to hang the peach color lace curtains I had made for the two pairs of windows, I suddenly heard this loud banging of a pot with a spoon.

I looked questioningly at Father who burst out laughing and

answered my silent question. Robert and Samuel had finished cooking and were calling our hungry band of hard workers to refreshment and temporary rest. With no running water in that area there were several wells in people's yards. There was a very large, well built one at the back of the high school, and when the students had heard the call to eat, they all rushed to the well. I looked lovingly over my brood as the boys pulled up buckets of water for the girls to wash their hands and faces, then took their turns. As they gathered on the grassy bank of the river behind Father's house each person was presented with a plate of hot food and a cup of water. I was truly happy and fulfilled at that moment and felt completely at peace in the realization that here was where I belonged.

CHAPTER SIX

Fathers Kwesi and Kofi did not directly participate in preparations for the reopening of the schools which was planned for early February, but they hovered at a safe distance. Sister D and I had decided that we would allow them to be a part of the school, but we would be the new administrators, as Bishop Henry had delegated. It was the tradition in Liberia for Catholic schools to set the pace - in education, in rules and regulations, even in uniform, and we in Greenville were not about to change that image, even though we found the school lacking in many areas.

My parents and the convent had trained me to give only of my best, so I was always pushing myself or being pushed to achieve excellence. I therefore did not accept half measures and did not expect it from those I worked with or those in my care. As I examined the staff of teachers I had inherited, I realized that I was stuck with not the cream of the crop as I would have expected but the scraps from the bottom of the barrel.

First of all, none of the seven male teachers was Liberian, and there were only two full-time ones. Most importantly, their capabilities as educators left much to be desired. The science tutor had the habit of excusing himself in the middle of a class, jumping on his bicycle, and riding off to get a "fix." This he did several times a day! When he returned he would mow, through the students especially the female ones, insulting and abusing them and reducing them to tears. Several of them had complained to Father Kwesi but he continued to ignore the situation. The history tutor taught word for word from the textbook never pausing to explain or give his own thoughts. When the students interrupted to question or comment, he pointedly told them to shut up! On and on the list went, and wanting the best for my students, I did not feel obligated to put up with that anymore. Father had appointed Fred, a Liberian teacher, as the vice-principal. He was the English tutor and renown for insulting students. He was extremely short and puny but he made up for this in arrogance and insolence. I was told that he had been a student in the seminary many years ago but was thrown out because of his attitude. That I could understand after I met this man and I wasn't sure I could tolerate the fact that I had to work with him. As fate would have it, he resigned before my arrival because Bishop Henry had promised to send him to Rome to study. Fred preened his feathers and lorded it over the other teachers, the parishioners, and especially the parish catechist. But everyone knew Bishop Henry and his promises, so they waited for the day that Fred would leave Liberia for Rome, but it never came.

In the junior school, Sister D was making similar discoveries about her brood and she, too, did not think it right. We therefore displayed posters advertising for teachers and inviting all well-qualified individuals to apply. Both priests were indignant because they had their reasons for keeping certain individuals in the schools. Apparently, they "owed" certain of these teachers or did them "favors," so these individuals were imposed upon the students. When we suggested replacing the teachers who were unsuitable, we faced their ire, but Sister D and I did not budge in our determination to obtain the best teachers for our students. We faced tremendous opposition from the priests in every attempt we made thereafter to improve the environment or anything to do with the schools. After scanning applications and interviewing those whom we felt suitable, we made our choice for teachers, but still had to contend with some of the previous ones whom we could not replace for one reason or another.

Then the next project we worked on was the "book room." What a dreary hovel that was! Books were piled high on every inch of the floor and the few shelves along the walls, and covered with thick layers of dust and cobwebs. This immediately told us that they were hardly ever used. We consulted the fathers, especially Father Kofi, who had a desk in this area and used it as his office.

He revealed that indeed, many of the books had never been used, mainly because the teachers themselves could not read the contents. Armed with flashlights, dusters, and brooms we set to work. There were four French-styled windows along the walls, and once the books were cleared away from their paths and the glass panes were cleaned, it was amazing how much light penetrated and filled the room.

As we sorted through and did an inventory, we discovered that most of these books were material that were not suitable for the students. The sisters had collected castoffs from their high schools in the United States and taken them there, but if the teachers could not read them, how could they teach the children from them? No wonder so many remained untouched and unused. Nevertheless, we did find many sets of readers that were usable in the high school because I was going to teach the classes of english language, literature, and feverishly promote reading skills to my students. Since there was no storage area or library in the high school, I asked Sister D to store them there for me.

When the bishop announced that Father Kwesi was no longer to be the administrator of the high school, I had hoped to transform his office into a library/reading room, but so far he was still established there with his stuff all over the desk, shelves, and floor. I did not lose hope though, because he had told me that he was to return to Ghana in July, so I would improvise until then. In the meantime Sister D made a list of books she would need to order for use in the junior school, and I began to research foreign agencies to solicit funds for the construction of a library and a science laboratory, both of which St Joseph's sadly lacked. Sister D had her own funds which she was pouring into the school; I had none so I had to raise or solicit them.

During the last week of January we invited all students interested in attending St Joseph's to sit for an entrance examination. There was one for each grade - from kindergarten to grade twelve - and students turned up in droves. We were well aware of the practice of students "buying" grades from teachers, and even the Catholic school was not immune. To prevent this happening, Sister and I corrected all the papers ourselves so all the students received a fair grade which depended only on their aptitude.

We set our passing grade at 75 percent and made no exceptions. Again we experienced opposition from the priests. They were the ones who had set the ground rules but they were always breaking them to please some people whom they favored. I did not think this fair and so did not budge when they pressed me to accept students who had done very badly in the examination but were children of parish council members or who did "favors" for them. (I discovered soon after becoming involved in the school that both priests had countless girlfriends. I didn't approve, but I did not think I knew them well enough yet to speak with them about such matters. But I would as soon as I had won their friendship and confidence.) We met with all the teachers to set a timetable and to talk about lesson plans, then we took a moment to regain our equilibrium.

With almost everything up to our standards, we mustered up our courage and opened the schools at the beginning of February. That was 1990. Typically, the school day began at 7:30A.M. When the bell was rung, students formed lines according to their grades. They were led in prayer by the designated teacher or student. Even though we were a Catholic institution we did not deny anyone a proper education because of their religion but I set down one firm rule. Students knew that prayer was an important and essential part of our curriculum, so once they chose to attend our institution, they had to participate in all religious activities.

After the short prayer session, the student body would be addressed by the principal who would teach morals and wisdom to both students and teachers. Then, the students turned to face the flagpole while two students hoisted the national flag of the country. They then saluted their flag and recited the pledge or sang their national anthem. After random announcements, students marched class by class, in order of rank, into their classrooms to begin formal classes which included: English, literature, reading, religion, maths, history, geography, economics, science (biology, chemistry, physics) and singing.

Classes were forty-five minutes in duration and there was a thirty- minute break from 10:00 A.M. to 10:30 A.M. during which students were allowed to run free, scream, shout, play ball or partake of the goodies sold by the vendors who lined the school wall near the church. Vendors, mainly mothers of the students, prepared coconut candy, roasted peanuts, popcorn, rice or plantain bread and even "foo-foo" and soup.

For the first few weeks we observed that these vendors were allowed free reign in front of the church and always left an awful mess when recess was over, but Sister D and I soon fixed that. We held a meeting with them and had them elect a leader who would take the responsibility of collecting a fee of one quarter from each vendor and making sure that the area was cleaned up after they were finished. The alternative - they would be thrown off the mission. We had no more problems after that.

At the end of the break, a bell was rung to indicate the end of recess. The bell was rung two more times, and on the third ring students were supposed to be in their lines in front of the school ready to march into their classrooms. Classes resumed and continued until 2:00 P.M. Each class had a rooster for students to take turns cleaning the classroom, and this had to be done before 3:00 P.M. when the evening school began.

These evening sessions were arranged for students who were late registering for the morning sessions and for female students who had become pregnant before completing their grade. Fred, the vice-principal of the high school, was the principal of this evening school, and while the priests suspected him of dishonesty, they never followed through. Sister D was elected to be the principal, but Fred refused to hand over anything to her. He was responsible for collecting the fees and banking them, but never gave an account of these funds to anyone nor, hand over the ledger when it was requested.

So as not to deprive the students, the evening school was allowed to continue but Sister D kept close tabs on Fred and his assistant, Sam. She registered the students and collected the funds, much to the consternation of Fred. I suggested that she go to the bank and investigate whether there was any money in the account for the evening school. In the meantime she opened a new account for the funds she had recently collected. Father Kofi was co-signee on the account with Fred so he accompanied Sister D to the bank.

When they checked the account, to their utter amazement and disbelief they discovered that thousands of dollars were missing. There were just a few hundred dollars left and this they quickly withdrew and deposited in the new account. A few days later, the bank manager informed us that Fred had attempted to withdraw the balance in the account, but it was too late, Father and Sister had already closed the account. Immediately a meeting was called and Fred and Sam were confronted. Fred blamed Sam and Sam blamed Fred. Sister D and I wanted to go to the police, but the Fathers pleaded and advised us to set up a plan for the two thieving men to pay back the amount they had stolen. I was dead set against this, but the priests remonstrated and advocated that we should show mercy instead of making enemies. We agreed to let them pay back the amount, but their positions in the school were promptly terminated.

The evening session was organized in similar fashion to the morning session. There were grades one to nine, and numbers varied from two students to twenty. I taught French, English and religion to grades five to nine, while Sister D taught the other grades that had students. The hours of the school was from 3:00 P.M. to 5:30 P.M. because there was Mass in the church at 6:00

P.M. This meant that one of us had to go to the clinic to collect Sr. Angela and bring her to the church. When we first started, there would be only the three of us at Mass, but pretty soon we encouraged the students and some of the adults to attend.

Occasionally, during the school day, the priests invited us for lunch, but more often than not we went through the day without eating. We therefore anticipated going home to a warm meal. Even though it wasn't fancy, it was adequate and it was more familiar than the African dishes to which we had not yet grown accustomed. We had inherited Ben, the old man who had served the sisters before us. He filled the water barrels from the well that was near the clinic, cleaned the house, washed our clothes, kept the grass low around the house, and lit the coal pot when it was time for us to get home.

We had also inherited the watchdog for the sisters before us. She had an unusual name, and when we inquired the origin, Sister Fran had explained. The locals had never seen a German Shepherd and when they beheld her massive size they declared: "Sister, she beeg-O!" So Beego she was promptly named. She was penned up all day, and once let out in the evening no one could leave or enter the convent grounds. She ate only the local brown rice and the dried fish prepared by the Fanti people. I was terrified of Beego and therefore did not venture near her. To me she was a miniature donkey. When she stood she was taller than I was (and I was five feet five inches) and she had a fierceness that respected no one - not even the sisters. Ben was responsible for cooking her special food, cleaning her pen, and bathing her once a month.

After Mass, Sisters Angela, Doris and I would drive into town to buy fresh bread and other grocery items, then back to the convent. We were a lot more relaxed on the mission, so we did not remain formally clothed in the religious garb. Some time later, we proceeded to our chapel to pray our Evening Prayer, the prayer recited by all the nuns.

Our chapel was now inside the convent. Since we did not

intend to do any entertaining, we transformed the small sitting room just inside the front door into a chapel. We removed the Blessed Sacrament (the tabernacle Catholics use to house the Sacred Host, which is believed to be the actual presence of Christ) from the sisters' old chapel, which was the palavar hut outside the convent, and placed it on a table against the back wall of the room. Then we placed chairs in two semicircles in front of the tabernacle. Our new chapel had to be consecrated, so we asked Father Kwesi to celebrate Mass. After that, Mass was celebrated every Wednesday, and the priests joined us for supper and recreation during which we played card and other board games.

After Evening Prayer, Sisters Angela, Doris, and I sat around the kitchen for a very informal supper and shared our day's activities and experiences. The three of us were thrown together for the first time, although I had lived in communities briefly with each of them separately. When I was living at the Mother House attending the seminary, Sister Doris was a novice in the same convent which was also the novitiate, but I was so busy and her schedule was so different that we never really communicated much.

Sister Doris was a unique nun. She had led a full, complete family life but after her spouse died and her children grew up she fervently desired to live the life of a nun. She was unconditionally and unquestionably accepted and even though she was over sixty years old, she was only five years a nun. I greatly admired her courage in freely abandoning the full, beautiful life she had led. Her deep faith and sincere devotion were dauntless. While she subjected everyone to her matriarchal qualities, which some of the nuns found overbearing, I found her to be extremely kindhearted, compassionate, and generous. She possessed a mountain of patience which I thought she could never lose, but I soon discovered that she could be stern and even "hard-hearted" when the occasion arose.

Sister Angela was a trained nurse, but surprisingly found

herself in teaching situations for most of her religious life. She worked mainly with the handicapped and was the sister in charge of one of the institutions the sisters administrated when I was sent to live in her community for a while in order to seek medical treatment at the nearby hospital for my stomach. She was extremely kind to me, taking time from her school work to drive me to the hospital and make sure that I rested as the doctor ordered. She was also in her sixties, but belonged to the "old school" of nuns. She was one of those older nuns who constantly criticized the younger nuns and gave them little encouragement or credit for anything they did.

I had never been close to Sister Angela, I did not hate her but I was wary of her. I had the strong feeling that she was constantly "watching" me, waiting for me to fail. I didn't think I deserved that kind of scrutiny thousands of miles away from my family and friends, but I walked on eggshells so as not to rub her the wrong way. As our days passed, to my utter surprise I discovered that she and Sister Doris did not see eye-to-eye on many things. There were periods when neither of them spoke to each other and Sister Angela would approach me to speak to Doris and make peace.

At these times, when communication was at a low and tension was running high, Sister Doris and I would retreat to our rooms immediately after supper to prepare lessons for the next day. The teachers at both schools were unfamiliar with preparing lesson plans or using them in the classroom. This was one of the things sister and I insisted upon, so we had the teachers practice writing the plans which we corrected over and over until they would become adept at them. Then sister had to prepare her lessons for kindergarten while I prepared for the classes I taught - English, literature, reading, religion, French and singing.

Sister Doris assumed the responsibility of checking the lesson plans of the teachers in the junior school and occasionally spot-checking their teaching sessions. This should have been the responsibility of Francis, the principal but we all knew he could not be trusted one bit. Francis was a sleazy shrimp of a man with the most lecherous, evil sneer on his face. He gave the impression that he had power over the fathers and attempted to laud it over us, but immediately backed off when I put him in his place.

What he lacked in size he made up for in arrogance and obnoxiousness. He took advantage of the students, especially the female ones whom he blackmailed and used for his own ends. The one thing that crowned my aversion for him was the fact that he relished the task of flogging the students mercilessly. He would turn students -- both male and female -- over desks and flog them for the most petty things. One day I asked Father Kwesi why Francis was allowed to continue with this wanton behavior, and Father nonchalantly replied, "Well, sister, if that makes him feel powerful let him boost his morale, but the students don't like or respect him one bit." I counted the days to the arrival of Sister Monica who would assume the principalship from him. I waited to watch his overinflated ego become deflated.

While rumors of war penetrated the towns and trickled in to us, we kept the school open and classes continued as usual. During the first week of April, just before Easter, Father Kwesi decided that since he would soon be leaving the school and I would assume full responsibility of the students and their affairs, I needed to learn my way around, so he took me on a trip to Monrovia. The day we planned to fly to Monrovia we could not get a flight together, so I went on the first flight that had a vacant seat. Actually, this seat was in the cockpit with the pilot. I was timid at first, but William, one of the two Liberian pilots, soon set me at ease. When he leaned over and allowed me to take the wheel and "fly" the plane for a few minutes I was exhilarated and descended from that experience convinced that I wanted to be a pilot.

I arrived in Monrovia around midafternoon and took a cab to the convent where I was to stay. All the sisters were out at their respective jobs so I left my bag with Brother Roland, one of the

Salesian brothers who had a school next to the convent, and headed to the shopping area downtown. As I ventured further into the city I noticed a lot of armed soldiers wandering around the streets. People were doing business as usual but a sense of urgency and tension prevailed. The presidential palace, under exceptionally heavy guard, was situated right opposite the University of Liberia.

As I perused the shops, I overheard bits and pieces of fearful conversation about the political situation in the city. Feeling unsafe and a bit scared, I returned to the convent. By this time the sisters had returned, and as I greeted them I shared my experience and asked them for news. They were uncertain of the situation but remained calm for the time being. After sharing an evening meal I retired for the night, for the next day I would go to the airfield to see if Father Kwesi had been fortunate enough to get a flight out of Greenville.

I was up early next morning and as I headed out to Spriggs Payne Airfield in a taxi I could only hope and pray that Father Kwesi would soon arrive. As I waited, I was joined by Thomas, a parishioner from Greenville who worked on the port there and sometimes in Monrovia. He had intercepted a message on the CB radio that I was to be informed that Father Kwesi was on a plane heading for Monrovia. He went to the convent, but when the sisters informed him that I had already left for the airfield, he headed straight out there.

Thomas waited with me until Father arrived, then he took us in his jeep, first to a local "cook shop" for lunch, then to the rectory where Father Kwesi would stay. Thomas informed Father and me that he was available to take us wherever we needed to go. Father Kwesi asked him to drive us to the Department of Education where I was introduced to the staff. The office for the West African Examination Council was also housed there, and I would have to go there to register future twelfth and ninth grade students for that examination. Again, I turned a blind eye as Father passed around the dollar bills. Everyone greeted Father and me like old friends.

When we left the office and went back to the jeep where Thomas was waiting, he informed us that he had been unexpectedly called back to duty on the port and was sorry to have to leave us. Father thanked him for all his help and told him he was free to go. Father had other errands to run, and I wanted to visit the shops at the waterside market, so we decided to walk. As we approached the marketplace Father and I were arguing about the practice of freely handing out money. "Ah, sister, you are new but after a few months you will have to do it to get by," Father said. "No, Father, I totally disagree. I'm sorry, but I will be the exception!" I hotly countered.

Just then a little boy who looked no more than six or seven approached me selling perfume. Ironically, the one he held out for me to test was named "Exception!" This coincidence dissipated my anger and made me burst out laughing. I asked the boy how old he was and he proudly declared: "Ten years of age!" When we inquired the price of the perfume he was selling, he said the largest bottle of "Exception" cost ten Liberian dollars but after haggling, I was able to purchase it for three. To this day, "Exception" remains my favorite perfume.

As we continued our journey on foot, Father, who was extraordinarily perceptive, sensed that trouble was brewing so he suggested we curtail our errands and return to the convent and rectory. For once I did not argue with him, (he lifted an eyebrow and asked if I was okay because we were always disagreeing and forever arguing about everything -- from Church doctrine to student affairs to personal beliefs). Instead I joined him in an effort to secure a cab to take us home. Suddenly there was a hail of gunfire and everyone began rushing in the opposite direction, sweeping us away in the force.

Father hailed a cab and when it stopped I was shoved in along with about ten other people. When I looked, Father was not among them. When the cab sped off I saw Father on the side of the road waving good-bye. Then more shots rang out, and my last sight was of him running for cover. I arrived back at the convent safely, but I worryied about him until he called later in the evening to say that he had reached the rectory without incident. We then made plans to fly back to Greenville the next day. Needless to say, the only way we were able to secure seats together on a flight was by producing the necessary extra dollars.

CHAPTER SEVEN

We returned to Greenville to find a very chaotic scene. First, the school had been burglarized. Some person, or persons, had cut a hole in the roof of the book room and entered. Father Kofi had a tin with money there but it was all stolen. Then, several parents, alarmed by the news trickling into Greenville from Monrovia, had removed their children from the school and taken them to hide in the bushes. To crown matters, there was a radio message that Theresa, Father Kwesi's cousin who was a nurse in Ghana, was arriving in a few days to visit him.

Father was bewildered and angered by this news at this particular time but there was no way to convey a message to her that her visit was bad timing. As tension mounted, all we could do was prepare for her visit and await her arrival. When she arrived in Monrovia she was met by a Ghanaian priest in the diocese. She was then put on a flight to Greenville, and soon she was welcomed to the mission house where she was to stay. Theresa was around my age and very shy, so we soon became fast friends. She loved the ocean as much as I did and so every free opportunity I had I organized picnics to the port area where we explored the many beautiful coves along the coast.

Despite the mounting aura of fear and tension, Father Kwesi insisted on continuing school sessions. He was looking for a challenge or an adventure, and I could tell that his decision was based on the fact that he wanted to be in the thick of things when the action occurred. So we busied ourselves with classes and caring for the kids who remained for the time being but we were worried by the news reports coming in on BBC and Voice of America. Then in the midst of all of that, when we least expected it, word came that our luggage left back in England would be arriving on a ship in Monrovia in a few weeks' time. We were elated because we thought we would never see those things again.

The message requested that one of the sisters be present at the port in Monrovia to receive the crate, process the paperwork, and make arrangements for it to be shipped to the port of Greenville. For once this was perfect timing. Theresa was supposed to return to Ghana the next week, and Father Kwesi was hoping to drive her to Monrovia so she could see that part of the country she hadn't had a chance to visit. Father immediately decided that I should be the one to go and clear the crate and so suggested that I make the journey with them. We were to be joined by Betty, the choir mistress of the church, and Frances, the wife of the parish council president who were both journeying to Monrovia to conduct business.

At precisely 3:00 A.M. on the Monday of the next week, Father Kwesi, driving the white Corolla car that was the priests' and accompanied by Theresa, Betty, and Frances, drove into the yard of the convent. I was well prepared and waiting for him, because knowing his impatience, if I was not ready he would either toot the horn and wake the two sisters or drive off and forget about me!

I had prepared to spend at least one week in Monrovia so I carried a small overnight bag as well as the sandwiches I had made for all of us and a flask of hot coffee. I quickly joined the traveling party occupying the front seat which was left vacant for me. The three women occupied the spacious back seat surrounded by a mountain of bags and packages. As Father swung out of the convent yard I opened the car window a crack and was greeted by a waft of the cold spring breeze.

The air was thick with the mist of the "Hammaton." This was early May and we were in the "Hammaton" season, which is the equivalent of spring. The mist is actually sand from the Sahara which drifts and sits like a huge cloud over the entire country. While this cloud rests over the area, it is exceptionally cold for a country so close to the Equator. Seeing the older folks wrapped from head to toe in their "lappas" or the more fashionable arrayed in coats, sweaters, ponchos, and the like, was not amusing when we ourselves experienced the cold piercing through our light clothing and chilling us to the bones. We too resorted to wearing sweaters at that time.

As we drove on I sucked in the air fragrant with the scent of the blossoms that lined the dirt road as well as the smell of freshly cut trees timbered by the various logging companies as they cleared their particular parts of the forest. Father refused the coffee and sandwiches which were being passed around and instead chose to chew "Kola" nuts. These nuts are extremely bitter and possess certain narcotic qualities which make the eater extremely alert and energetic. When consumed in large quantities, they have the same effects as marijuana, but eaten moderately they keep you awake, alert, and without any desire for food for hours. Father Kwesi was by no means a timid driver, so with the car stereo blaring and his full concentration on the road, he cleared the miles that stretched ahead with a reckless speed.

The first town we stopped in was Zwedru. At the first checkpoint we did not have to endure the usual rigorous and sometimes embarrassing searching of vehicles, stripping of persons, and even illegal removal of goods. Their faces lit up as Father approached and passed around a wad of bills. We drove slowly through the town and life seemed normal. But, when we arrived at the checkpoint to leave that town, chaos reigned.

A large crowd of people were milling around. There was desperation on people's faces. The soldiers demanded that we descend and our bags searched. As usual, Father Kwesi offered monetary appeasement. We suffered no indignity of a bodily "frisk" but we did not escape so lightly when we attempted to drive off. The chief soldier demanded that Father allow an armed soldier and a female passenger laden with bags to join us. We protested but it fell on deaf ears. We had to take these two strangers or we would be detained.

The women at the back made themselves small so as to accommodate the female passenger while the soldier, no more than a boy, opened the front door and jumped in, landing unceremoniously on top of me. I pushed him away, yanked my arm and leg from beneath his weight, and scooted as far away from him as I could. He reeked of sweat and alcohol and my whole being revolted. He was in such a stupor he did not realize that I had pushed him so hard he was hanging out the side of the car. Another soldier caught him before he fell out, pushed him back inside, and closed the car door.

As we drove off I heard the women questioning the female passenger. The stranger identified herself as Rose and claimed she was from Nigeria. She was traveling to Monrovia to assume the responsibility of head nurse at the government hospital there. Theresa quickly said that she was also a nurse, and when she attempted to discuss nursing matters, Rose grew very nervous and evasive. She claimed she had a headache and wanted to take a nap so Theresa, with a baffled look, left her alone.

As her eyes were closed, I turned around and inspected Rose. She was quite attractive, very fashionably dressed, and had a good command of the English language. But what caught my attention was a quaint bracelet and necklace set she wore. It appeared to be made of some sort of dried grass and had a most peculiar odor. I had many questions, but they would have to wait. We had reached the next large town, Tappita. To my utter relief, as the car stopped, the soldier seemed to spring to life. He flung open the door, jumped out, and ran towards the village.

We all descended except Rose. While we explored the terrain and sought a spot to "water," she remained seated, head laid back eyes closed. Once we were out of earshot I voiced my suspicions about Rose and the strange paraphernalia that adorned her. Frances said, "Don't worry, sister, that's just her "zangalay goa!" "Her what?" I naively queried.

Frances, Betty and Theresa burst out laughing. Father Kwesi was attracted by the peals of laughter and came over and started poking fun at me when Betty explained, "Sister doesn't know what a zangalay goa is; tell her Father!" Father stroked his face like a wise old sage and replied, "Well sister, you ever heard of joo joo? Having grown up in the Caribbean I was familiar with "obeah," which was one form of the practice of evil, so I nodded.

Frances then went on to explain that a "zangalay goa" was an evil artifact or "medicine" prepared by the medicine man orwoman and worn in various parts of the body for many different reasons. The wearer's aim was to gain a certain forceful power or influence over someone, or success in a task. For instance, a woman may wear one to win over the man of her heart, a football player may wear one to gain his team victory in an important game, or an individual may wear one to obtain a certain job. Some of these "charms" were prepared from simple, harmless but powerful herbs while others were concocted from more intricate materials. The most evil ones were those made from human bones ground into powder and sewn into a small pouch. When the school had been reopened, I noticed almost all the students wearing some sort of peculiar bracelet or scrap of string around their necks.

Father Kwesi had warned me not to touch any of these or force the students to take them off, but I had a plan. We had a rule against wearing jewelry to school so I fined each student who wore one of these artifacts. Soon I had a large tin in my office full of the "zangalay goas" (usually a nickel or dime) and the students remained unharmed, thus proving that there was absolutely no power in these pieces of string and cloth.

We returned to the car and when we resumed our journey I invited everyone to pray the rosary. Suddenly Rose's head reared up and she declared that she didn't want any noise. I was tempted to tell her that she had only pretended to be asleep but I bit my tongue, ignored her, and began the prayers, while the others joined in. Father asked her if she was afraid of the prayers, and she declared that she was not because she was a Catholic too. Father immediately challenged her, "Okay, prove it, make

91

the sign of the cross!" The way she crossed herself was not the sign of the cross, and this further proved the web of deceit she wove.

We reveled in the peace that pervaded the car. Each was deep in thought when Father entered the town called Sannequille. Suddenly, without warning, we were confronted by a surge of army trucks racing in the opposite direction. As they sped by us I could see in the trucks soldiers well and alive and soldiers very dead. The soldiers who were driving blared their horns, flashed their lights, and signaled us with their flailing arms to turn back.

Father Kwesi kept driving on, but when Theresa grew hysterical, leaned over, and pulled the wheel from his hands, he was forced to spin the car around. He began screaming at her in their Ghanaian dialect, scolding her and calling her a coward. I retorted that he was being stupid and would get us all killed. But, being the challenge-seeking man of God he was, he went forward to investigate what was happening. As he kept shouting at Theresa she began to cry and made to open the car door and jump out. That brought him back to reality and he quickly relented. He stopped the car, calmed Theresa, and we all let out their breath.

Father pondered, uncertain what to do, but knowing that we had to get to Monrovia because Theresa had a plane to board to return home. Restarting the engine Father slowly guided the car in the opposite direction. We drove a short distance and there, on our right, was a large gate closing off a narrow dirt road. No one said anything because we had no idea where it led. Father stopped abruptly and addressed the man standing guard. "Da wah, na fweh wah!" which was the Kru for "Good morning." The man responded in English so Father continued.

"Please, sir, you have to let us through. The Sister is very ill and I have to get her to the JFK Hospital." To support his story, I leaned forward clutching my stomach, my face distorted in pain. The poor man was duped because he opened the gate without hesitation and let us through. The women were amused and Frances reprimanded him, "Eh-ya, Father, I never know the priest could tell lie too. Now you have to go to confession!" Father cockily replied that it was a "white lie" to save our lives and concentrated on maneuvering the treacherous, winding path ahead.

Father suddenly gained momentum and pitched the car forward at a reckless speed. I tried to coax him to slow down but my pleas fell on deaf ears. Observing him, I realized that his adrenaline was overflowing, so the best thing to do was just to let him burn it off. I sat back quietly, tightly clutching my rosary, and prayed quietly. A few miles and almost an hour later my prayers were answered.

There was a loud bang that sounded like a gun shot, and the car skidded to a stop. Father got out to investigate and discovered a flat tire. We welcomed the time of rest, and while the women searched out the bushes I assisted Father to change the flat. Father stomped around and told the women to hurry or he would leave without them.

We all still regarded Rose cautiously but Theresa, Betty, and Frances were much more civil to her now. Chatting like old friends, they paid no mind to Father and his bad mood and took their time boarding the car. This further aggravated Father, but they simply ignored him.

I put my head back on the headrest and closed my eyes and just as I was dozing off, there was another loud bang. Father pulled aside and began to swear. The spare had blown out so now we had two tires that needed repairing. Mumbling and swearing to no one in particular, he removed the one damaged tire from the wheel and the other from the car trunk. He commanded us to stay put, placed both tires on his head and began his trek to find a village where he could get them repaired.

Darkness slowly descended on us. We sat in the car and listened intently to the eerie silence around us. We seemed to be in the middle of nowhere. Betty and Frances wanted to walk around and explore the area but Theresa advised them against it. Father had been gone for more than four hours and we were all concerned and growing restless. The women began asking me questions about where I came from, my family, the convent and every aspect of my life as a nun. I didn't really know them and was too shy to readily make friends so this gave me an opportunity to open up to them.

As I was relating a story about some of the nuns, we felt eyes watching us. It was an eerie, terrifying feeling but we were not imagining things. As we surveyed our surroundings, the car was encircled by a group of children in different stages of nakedness and with faces painted white. I was scared to hell but Frances soothed my frayed nerves by explaining that these boys and girls were quite harmless. They were attending a "Bush School" somewhere nearby which meant that there was a village not far away.

Frances and Betty spoke to the children in every different dialect they were familiar with but the children didn't respond. That was mainly because we were in a county that spoke a completely different dialect, unfamiliar to the women. The children seemed undaunted that we couldn't communicate but they appeared to understand our plight. They began to sing and dance and did indeed form a fine entertainment troupe. Meantime Frances, Betty and Theresa enlightened me about a "Bush School."

Once a boy or girl reached puberty it was the norm of the village society to hold a "bush" or "Zoe" school. The women explained that each person had a different description of what actually occurred during this time because it was supposed to be very secret and the participants were not supposed to talk about what they were subjected to. Stories, however leaked out because not everyone refrained from sharing the secrets.

When a girl reached the age of ten or eleven she joined other girls her age or older to be trained to be proper African wives. The new member is never told where she was being led as she was tricked and taken to the hut which housed the school. The very frightening and horrific ritual of "female circumcision" was performed on the girls by a woman specially chosen from the village. The sole purpose of this mutilating operation was for the young girl to remain completely pure and untainted until her wedding night.

As the young girl is taken to the hut under deception, the woman waited with a brand new razor. The girl's mother, elder sisters and female cousins would also be there. They would physically subdue the girl while the woman proceeded to slice off part of her genital then sew the cavity that had been created leaving only a tiny hole for urination and monthly bleeding. That whole operation was performed under very unhygienic conditions and without any form of anesthetic so the victim violently screamed and fought as she endured immense pain.

Needless to say several problems arose from this procedure. There were the physical scars and complications. Some girls had been killed as they bled to death or succumbed to the overwhelming pain. Then there were the emotional scars. Because of the betrayal by the person who had led the girl to the hut, she remained distrustful of that person and everyone else associated with the ceremony. The boys, housed separately, were having their turns being tried, tested, tortured and humiliated in order to prove themselves ready for manhood.

At the end of the "school" there was some sort of ceremony where the boys and girls were allowed to meet and choose mates. Once the girl was chosen for marriage, she underwent another stage of training and preparation for her marriage. The stitches from her sewed up private part were only removed the day of the wedding. Because of the discomfort caused by that operation the girls never enjoyed their womanhood as they were supposed to. Sister Angela encountered several cases of that form of mutilation when the women came to the clinic to be examined but they would never tell exactly what had happened to them. I was totally appalled by that story but the women assured me that not all villages practiced that ritual.

It had now grown completely dark and we were hungry, tired and concerned about the whereabouts of Father Kwesi. The children also seemed tired as they stopped performing for us and stood still for a while. Soon one of the girls who must have been about twelve years and seemed like the leader of the group signaled that they wanted to push the car along the road. Betty, Frances and Theresa alighted from the car to help push while I got into the driver's seat to steer but then I realized that I was not alone. Madam Rose refused to get out and help but stayed put in the back seat. I was angry with her but too tired and scared to scold or argue with her. I asked that they push the car gently because we were rolling on three tires and one bare rim.

We rolled along for about five miles when we came to a sign at the side of the road. It read "Boys Town" and stood at the entrance of a driveway leading to a large concrete house. We could see flickering lights all around and in the distance which indicated that we were in the midst of a large village. The car was guided into the yard and as I opened the door and stepped out I created quite a stir. I was fully clothed in my religious habit and veil.

I looked around observing the open stares when an old but stately looking man stepped forward and spoke to me in perfect English. He identified himself as the village chief and invited us to stay and partake of their hospitality. I thanked him and explained our plight. He summoned his eldest wife and requested her to find sleeping quarters for us to spend the night. Betty, Frances and Theresa were to share a room in a house next door to the chief's house while his wife invited me to stay in their house.

Rose had not shown her face as yet and I would have gladly let her sleep in the car but simple charity made me point out to the chief that there was another traveler who remained in the car because she was unwell. He was in a quandary because he did not know where she could stay but I quickly assured him that she could share the room I was to occupy. My skin crawled as I thought of spending the night in the same room with one so deceitful, strange, unlikeable and grouchy but I knew I had to set a good example so it took all my willpower to accomplish that task.

I decided to wait awhile in the car in case Father Kwesi returned. Each time I heard a vehicle approaching I flashed the car lights so he would recognize the car. After waiting an hour the women wanted to go to bed and asked if they could take a shower. The chief's wife sent one of the boys to fetch buckets of water from the nearby well while she heated a pot on the fire lit in the middle of her kitchen. When Betty, Frances and Theresa had their turns Theresa offered to sit in the car and keep watch while I took a shower.

I had seen the roughly constructed outdoor bathrooms as I walked pass people's houses in Greenville but it was the first time I was using one. It was made with several sheets of zinc galvanize wired together and securely tied to four posts buried in the earth. Either planks of wood or slabs of stone covered the dirt inside the enclosure where one stood to shower. There was neither roof nor door but that did not matter because the night was pitch black.

Armed with towel, soap and a clean garment to change into I was led to the bathroom by the boy carrying the bucket of water in one hand and a lantern in the other. He hung the lantern on a tree nearby so I could use it to find my way back. Thus under the star filled sky I experienced my first open air, outdoor shower. I returned a few glorious minutes after feeling renewed from that lukewarm shower. I asked Rose if she wasn't going to take a shower and she replied that she wasn't ready yet. I scolded her for making the boy have to return to draw water whenever she was well and ready to take a bath but she ignored me.

Around ten o'clock I told the women to go to bed while I stayed up and kept watch for Father Kwesi's return. Rose said that she would wait with me and I didn't argue while the other three eagerly walked across to the house where they were to sleep. I had dozed off when shortly after midnight I faintly heard a vehicle approaching. I quickly flashed the car lights until the vehicle abruptly stopped and I heard Father's voice declare: "Da ma car-O, da ma car!" As I opened the car door and stepped out I saw Father alighting from a beat up old pick up truck. He lifted the two tires off the truck, paid the driver and stalked over to his car.

I greeted him and began to ask about his journey but he brushed me aside and bent down to replace the tire on the bare wheel while stubbornly insisting that we leave immediately. The villagers gathered around the car offering to help him and advising that he spend the rest of the night and depart early the next morning. At that point Father seemed too exhausted to argue so he agreed. When I saw his determination relax, I asked the boy to draw water for Father to take a bath. By the time he was finished mounting the repaired tire and asked for water to bathe, it was all ready for him.

The three women had heard the commotion and came out to see what was happening. The four of us were standing at the side of the car when lo and behold, our friend Rose alighted and declared: "I think I will take bath now!" I just forgot who I was and where I was. In a fit of temper I demanded if she had no shame, if she had no respect for the priest or herself and if she had designs on Father Kwesi she had better get them out her mind. The three women, realizing what Rose had intended to do, tore at her with sharp, biting words that made her storm out of our presence and head for the house where she was to sleep. Frances and Theresa began to tease me telling me that she was going to work her "joo joo" on me while I slept because I had foiled her plans to entangle Father in her web. I assured them that I would be all right and sent them back to sleep.

When I attempted to enter the house to sleep for the few hours left, the door was locked and realized that Rose had done it. I knocked lightly so as not wake everyone and soon a little girl came and let me in. Thank God there was a chair in one corner of the room. I curled up there and prayed the rosary over and over until I saw signs of day break. Father had chosen to sleep in the car so I dressed quickly and went to wake him as well as Betty, Frances and Theresa. By four a.m. we were ready to resume our journey and after thanking the chief, his wife and the villagers for their hospitality, we drove off.

As we ambled on still in the middle of nowhere everyone was very subdued but no one commented. I was totally exhausted and terribly hungry. I had not slept a wink and ached all over from not having stretched out for the night. but I wasn't about to complain. Rose had donned a very elaborate outfit and had sprayed herself excessively with a very offensive smelling cologne. All the car windows were rolled right down to let in fresh air and drive out the pungent odor. Father turned on the car stereo and begun to hum along with the tune playing while I laid my head back on the seat and dozed.

I was suddenly awakened and almost jumped out of my skin in terror when I heard a loud bang and the car swerved. After recovering from the shock and realizing that we had not been shot at, I could not believe it. Another tire had blown out. Father angrily stopped the car and got out to change it and when he checked the other three found that the left front one was losing air which meant that it had a hole. There we were again sitting at the side of the road while Father removed both tires and began his trek to find someone to repair them.

As the five of us sat in the car I could see Theresa's suspicions about Rose surfacing. She began to question Rose with a severity that made Rose cringe and soon she broke and spilled her story. With a sly smile and an air of confidence she explained that she was married and had a ten year old son but that her husband had left her a few months before and taken her son with him. They lived in Monrovia and he worked at the JFK Hospital but she was going to fix that. She had obtained the medicine and was on her way to Monrovia to retrieve her son and to "steal" her husband's job.

Her face was contorted with the ugliest, most evil expression as she described how she was going to walk into the hospital, wearing her special charm bracelet and necklace and conquer everyone and everything she set out to do. Theresa openly exclaimed: "Aha, I knew it!" The rest of us were too shocked by what we had just heard. I had heard of the charms, potions and spells people could use to evil ends but never had I come so close to any of them as I was then. I opened the car door and said I was going for a walk. I walked and walked until I came upon a creek on the side of the road. I walked down and sat on the bank. Those few moments of solitude, observing the flowing water helped calm my fears and the sense of evil that had engulfed us. Soon I heard footsteps and when I turned around I noticed Betty, Frances and Theresa approaching.

Whilst they were not shocked or mildly surprised at the bombshell that had just been dropped on us by Rose they were angry and upset that she took advantage of us and even had us fooled especially Father Kwesi. I asked where she was and they said they after I left they all decided to go in search of a village where they could prepare a meal for us. She said she didn't want to go so they told her to stay and watch out things. I told them that I wasn't exactly fooled by her because I sensed the evil that surrounded her. From the time she had joined our traveling party every time I was alone with her I broke out in goose bumps and that always happened when I sensed evil nearby.

We continued talking for a while each formulating a plan to find a way for Rose to continue the journey by other means. The hardest part would be to convince Father Kwesi of her web of deception. I suddenly felt the urge to get under the water in the creek. The sun was blisteringly hot, I was hungry, tired, scared and desperately felt the need to "drown my sorrows". I had spent two days with these three women either cooped up in a car driving or stranded at the side of the road and had overcome my shyness and shared very deeply with them while they in turn spoke openly to me about very intimate things in their lives. I felt comfortable enough to voice my desire to go for a swim even though I didn't have a bathing suit.

When I did tell the women that I wanted to swim but I didn't have a suit they all laughed at first then Frances said I shouldn't worry she had the solution and I should definitely not feel bashful because they were all going to join me for a swim. Frances went back to the car and returned with one of her lappas. She directed me to take it, head for the bushes, take off all my clothes and wrap myself in it. I did as directed and soon returned securely wrapped in the lappa, hair loose and flowing down my back. The women were nowhere in sight but I heard their voices a little way off. I presumed they were preparing themselves for swimming so I quickly dove into the water and stayed under a while enjoying the exhilarating sensation of the water totally engulfing me and the peace it brought. When I surfaced I lay back on my back, eyes closed and floated but was suddenly roused when I heard a loud gasp.

I looked up expecting to see some wild animal stalking the women but instead was confronted by the three of them staring at me. I jumped up and ran out of the water to query their petrified countenances. "What's the matter?" I worriedly questioned the women. Frances moved forward, lifted my hair in her hands and declared teasingly: "Eh Sister, you scared us, you look just like a Mamie Water-O". "And who or what is Mamie Water?" I asked, annoyed that they had disturbed the deep peace I was enjoying with one of their superstitious beliefs which I was convinced this was.

Frances began to explain that when a Liberian drowned in the sea or river or any large body of water, they did not believe it was a natural death. They believe that there was a sea witch who lived in the water and who they believed had long flowing hair like mine. She roamed around the water when she needed to be appeased and took away the spirits of persons whom she caused to drown. I was infuriated by their beliefs that spirits ruled every aspect of a person's life but I was sensitive enough not to criticize or decry this belief. I assured them that I was no spirit but flesh and blood with feelings and needs. I facetiously warned them that if they did not hurry up and swim then find something for us to eat, I would eat one of them.

This broke the tension and soon we all jumped into the water, splashed around and had a grand time. I left the water first sat a while in the sun until I was completely dried then I dressed. After having their fill of the water they did the same and soon we were ready to return to the car and see what damages Rose had done. When we reached the car we saw her sprawled out in the back seat sleeping. That's exactly what I was hoping to do but she beat me to it and I made no comment. Theresa said that she had observed a box in the trunk that Father Kwesi was taking for a friend in Monrovia. She was going to open it because she felt it contained dried fish. Betty and Frances declared that they were afraid because Father would be sorely angry but Theresa was adamant. I told her to go ahead and I would say I opened it. I knew he would not dare yell at me no matter how much he would want to.

Opening it proved Theresa correct so they removed enough fish to boil and make pepper soup. I asked how they were going to cook this soup then Betty disclosed that on their way to the creek they had seen a path on one side of the road which they were sure led to a village. I gave them some money to purchase other foodstuff like rice, pepper, salt etc. and they were on their way. I was so tired and felt that if I didn't lie down I would faint. I removed my towel from my bag, found a shady spot under a tree, lay down and went fast asleep for what seemed like a month.

I was awakened by the women who returned bearing a potful of cooked rice, another of fish soup and a bundle of bowls and spoons. Frances set aside an ample serving of rice and soup for Father then served me in one of the bowls and Rose in another. Then pouring the rest of the soup into the pot which had the remainder of the rice the three of them proceeded to eat with their hands. I paused from my feast long enough to observe them enjoying their meal in such childlike simplicity and also to thank then profusely for the absolutely delicious meal they had prepared. Although I was not dipping and eating out of the same pot with them I felt such a sense of camaraderie with these three women. I felt guilty but I could not bring myself to like Rose or be warm toward her. I was polite and civil which I overextended myself to achieve but that was all she was going to get from me. I longed to be as far away from her as I could get and could not wait for Father Kwesi to return and find the solution to that. For the time being I just enjoyed my meal and the peace that had descended upon me.

After everyone had eaten their fill I told the three women that I would take the dishes down to the creek and wash up since they had prepared the meal so they made a bundle of the dirty dishes tied it in a lappa and placed it on my head. They began to tease and address me as "Kru 'Ooma'" the title given to a respected woman in the Kru community. In an effort to extend a hand of friendship to Rose I invited her to accompany me but she arrogantly claimed that she never washed dishes and besides she was too tired. I strode off elegantly balancing my bundle on my head, my resentment toward Rose growing by the second.

I washed the dishes and tied them back in the bundle just as Frances had done then placed it on my head and was returning to the car when I heard a vehicle approaching behind me. I stopped and stood by the edge of the path so it could pass freely but when it reached where I stood it stopped and Father Kwesi alighted, removed the two tires from the back of the truck, paid the driver and bade him good-bye. I also thanked the driver for bringing Father safely back to us. As the truck drove off I told Father I had serious matters to discuss with him and preferred talking before returning to the car. He patiently listened as I related the tale Rose had unfolded to us earlier that day.

As we neared the car, Frances, Betty and Theresa who were sitting under a tree saw us and came running. I informed them that I had told Father the story. I then turned and unleashed on him all my pent up anger, frustration, fear and all the other emotions that were eating at my insides as I sternly delivered an ultimatum - let her get a seat on any car, truck, bus, horse cart or anything moving in the direction of Monrovia or we would. He asked who the "we" was and Theresa, Frances and Betty spoke in unison declaring: "Us!" Theresa stepped forward and declared that Father should tell Rose that we had to make a detour stop on the mission in Buchannan to see a sick priest and that would deter her from arriving at the hospital on time.

Father stood, mouth open and eyes wide in surprise at my consternation and our confrontation. He knew that under normal circumstances those women would never stand up to him in such an blatant way. He knew very well that I was responsible since I had boldly but not disrespectfully confronted him, something an African woman would never dream of doing to an African man or any man for that matter. Both my parents had taught me to stand up for what was right and speak out against wrong, so I was doing just that!

Father realized then that he had a mutiny on his hands, that he was cornered and could not wiggle his way out of this one and so agreed to speak to Rose. We allowed him to go ahead and speak to Rose in private while we lingered behind. Frances was the first to reveal how surprised they were to hear me speak so forcefully to Father. I always appeared so shy, reserved and timid and they expressively admired the bold, brave, unabashed manner I had addressed Father on the subject of "Rose." Betty declared: "Yeh, Sister, you good to go!"

As luck would have it, as we walked leisurely back to the car we espied a vehicle approaching. We excitedly flagged it down and when it stopped I recognized the truck that had dropped off Father earlier on. We asked the driver to wait as we had a passenger for him. Theresa ran to the car and was in time to see

Rose gathering her stuff and repacking her bag. Theresa assisted her to complete the task and led her out to the truck. Room was made for her on the tray of the truck and hands reached out to help her up. Again, Father paid the driver and told him to take the lady safely to Monrovia.

As Rose left I walked off toward a nearby tree, sat down and burst into tears. I couldn't understand or explain why but it was as if a dam just burst inside of me. I silently analyzed myself and realized that this was part of my character. When faced with strong emotional situations like anger, fear or any form of stress I would stand firm, act brave and hold things together but the moment the tension was over, I sought solitude and broke. Some people shouted, screamed, threw things, used their fists or indulged in other forms of violence but I cried.

When I rejoined the others a few minutes after, Father gave me a peculiar look but refrained from commenting or teasing for once. Rose's departure made the air lighter. It was as if a weight had been lifted from everyone's shoulders and even from the car. Father had replaced the flat tire and eaten the meal that was left for him. He was so thankful for the women's thoughtfulness. As he ate we conversed freely about Rose's story, his journey's back and forth repairing tires and we all wondered aloud our concerns whether we would ever arrive in Monrovia. Father assured us that we would. Physically refreshed, mentally calmed and emotionally strengthened, the three women climbed into the back seat, I occupied the front seat and Father got behind the wheel to continue a journey we would never forget.

We arrived in Monrovia as dusk fell. The streets were unusually deserted and the number of checkpoints seemed to have increased since I had last visited the city. We could immediately feel the tension that filled the air. Father turned down the car stereo and his demeanor changed drastically. He grew stiff and silent and negotiated the roads extra cautiously and soon we arrived at the convent where I was to stay. I bade everyone farewell and Father reminded me that he was going to pick me up the next day around four p.m. because Theresa's flight was at six. He warned me not to go anywhere and be exposed to the dangers that seemed to lurk through the city.

The next morning dawned with brilliant sunlight streaming in through every crack and opening of the building. After Mass and breakfast I inquired about the safety of the city because I had an important errand to run. Brother Mark from next door informed me that he was riding into town and if I wanted I could ride with him. I accepted his offer and agreed to meet him in the school yard at ten a.m. The purpose of my errand was to use the opportunity to renew my Liberian driver's license. I had no idea where I had to go but I was certain Brother Mark would direct me. When I met Brother at ten o'clock I explained the reason for my journey into town and asked him to direct me where to go. He said that I had to go to the Police Headquarters and as he was going right past he would drop me off. The Police Headquarters was a new, elaborate building recently erected. As I ran instead of walking up the wide expanse of the front stairs into the foyer I could slice through with a knife the air that was thick with tension. The usual exuberant greetings and open spirit that characterized the locals were absent. Everyone seemed very subdued and wrapped up in their own worlds.

I quickly made my way to the office of the Director of Traffic and breathed a great big sigh of relief when I saw him sitting behind his desk. I anticipated spending an hour there for the most because I had already paid the required sum and had my picture taken in Greenville. All I had to do was present the receipt and be patient until they prepared the little "book" that would be stamped yearly when the license was renewed. I knocked on the office door and entered when invited. I stated the cause of my visit, produced the receipt and handed it to the man behind the desk. He quickly filled out two forms and after requesting that I sign them, demanded one hundred dollars. I asked what that money was for and he replied that it was his "fee". I adamantly stood my ground and declared that I was not paying one penny extra. The man looked at me in disdain and showed me out of his office.

I sat in a waiting room outside his office and waited. While I sat there I could hear sporadic outbursts of gunfire but I dared not ask what was happening because those who passed by hurried without making eye contact. I watched Mr. Director of Traffic leave his office at twelve o'clock and I presumed he was going to lunch and I was still sitting there when he returned at one p.m. He did not give me a second look as he sat behind his desk and acted as if I wasn't there. At three-thirty I saw him begin to clear his desk and I knew he was preparing to leave.

I went in and politely requested my driver's license. I controlling my resentment and mounting anger, I humbly pleaded, explaining that I was returning to Greenville city that night so that was my only opportunity to obtain the necessary document which was in his possession and besides I didn't have any large sum of money with me. The man remained unmoved and that provoked my peaceful countenance. I looked straight at him and sternly asked if I could the telephone to call Archbishop Mike. Archbishop Mike was part Liberian. He fully understood how these government officials harassed and took advantage of the foreigners and he constantly attacked them verbally for their unethical practices.

At the mention of Archbishop Mike's name the director's demeanor grew very nasty. He set his jaw, grit his teeth and threw the book across the desk at me. I saw the disdain on his face but I didn't care. I grabbed the license and ran out of his office. My only thought was of Father Kwesi going to the convent and not finding me because it was well after four p.m. I knew full well that I was going to experience his wrath for disobeying his directive to "stay put" so I raced down the steps and hailed a cab that was standing idle at the front of the building.

I immediately noticed that the cab did not have a meter therefore I had to bargain with the driver to give me a fair amount to pay to take me to Robertsfield airport which was over

107

forty miles away. I explained my predicament to the driver stating that I was late to catch a flight and he seemed quite familiar with that story. I sat at the edge of the seat and watched people, buildings, trees and other buildings melt and seem like small lights as we whizzed past. That journey which normally took one hour and a half was made in half the time - forty-five minutes. When I was safely deposited at the required terminal, I paid the driver handsomely, thanked him profusely swiftly mounted the stairs to the passenger lounge.

I immediately saw Theresa surrounded by a group of people I did not recognize as well as Betty, Frances and Father Kwesi. I ignored Father's stern look and concentrated on saying goodbye to Theresa. Theresa was sad to leave. She had grown very close to those friends who had gathered to bid her good-bye. She hugged me and declared that she was going to miss me very much. She pleaded with me to be careful and to bite my tongue in certain situations which may arise in the present state of the country.

I promised to be careful and waved frantically as she made her way toward the waiting aircraft. Once she was air borne, Father Kwesi turned to me. I had been ignoring him but now I had to face him. I quickly explained where I went and why I wanted to go without him. I knew that if he had been there he would have paid the sum demanded by the director of traffic and I wanted to prove that business could be achieved without that hateful practice of bribery.

As we headed back to the car, Elsa, one of the women who had gone to bid Theresa good-bye, invited us to dinner at her home. I had no idea who she was and I was in no frame of mind to socialize. I inquired from Father Kwesi who informed me that she was the mother of the young man who had become a football legend of Liberia and she had housed Theresa for the night she spent in Monrovia before arriving in Greenville. I didn't really care but I knew I had no choice but to be civil.

When we arrived at and entered her home I was pleasantly

surprised. She and her family lived in a very elaborate house fashionably furnished and I immediately noticed every wall and space plastered with pictures of her famous son who happened to be present and was the center of attention at the party being held in his honor. After exchanging greetings I conversed with him about his sport and he was surprised that I was so well informed about football until I explained that both my brothers were football players and I was always a big fan of the sport. The evening turned out to be quite pleasant and after partaking of the sumptuous dinner prepared we left the younger folk to party. As we made our way to the convent where I was dropped off, Father and I planned to visit the port the next day to get the matter of our luggage settled.

At the port the next day we didn't have any problems clearing the container that held our luggage. I signed the necessary papers and was given the name of the vessel that would transport the container from the port of Monrovia to the port of Greenville. Father handsomely rewarded the gentleman who attended to us so efficiently. He didn't charge us any fee and began to refuse the money Father handed him but when I asked him to accept it on behalf of the Sisters in gratitude, he did. When we left the office I asked Father to drop me into town because I wanted to look around the shops for a few things the sisters needed.

I was a bit nervous every so often there was sporadic gunfire and no one had any idea of the exact location. I knew he didn't have the patience to accompany me or wait on me while I shopped so I summed up the courage and proceeded to the shopping area but he let me on my own only after giving me a strong warning to be careful and promising to go straight back to the convent if anything happened. He informed me that we would depart Monrovia the next morning at the crack of dawn. I didn't object because I was actually eager to leave Monrovia which was rather unusual considering how much I loved that city and looked forward to spending as much time as I could there but not that one time.

The next morning Father Kwesi was at the convent gate at three a.m. for us to begin our journey back to Greenville. Only Frances was returning as Betty had remained to visit with relatives. We were informed that the road that had previously been blocked had been opened at midnight and if we chose to proceed through it we should be extremely cautious. I could see Father's eyes gleam with excitement when he realized that we would be the first to survey the area. We were warned that we might encounter some gruesome sights but Father was determined to see for himself. Surprisingly, he asked me if I had any objections and not wanting to appear cowardly, I retorted: "But why are we wasting so much time, shall we proceed?"

Father drove at his usual reckless speed until we left the town of Buchannan. We were now approaching the town of Sannequille, the place where we were turned back. This was the town through which Ray Harper and his band of rebels, the National Patriotic Front of Liberia, had entered Liberia from the Ivory Coast in his attempt to stage a coup. Father drove at a very leisurely pace and I could see him perspiring profusely as we surveyed the scene of death and destruction around us.

Frances began chanting a death wail and kept beating her breast and exclaiming: "Eh, ya!" Houses were burnt flat to the ground and there were dead bodies scattered in yards and at the side of the road. There were headless corpses, limb less corpses, dead women with dead babies on top of them, dead men and children all lying on their faces which meant that they were shot or killed with machetes from the back while they were fleeing.

I was appalled, angry and sad but I remained calm. I wanted to stop the car, gather up all the dead bodies and bury them then run after the animals who had committed such a heinous crime. Father held his balled up fist to his mouth and I could see his eyes shining with unshed tears. I could see the fear crawling over his body and I also knew he wanted to do something for those innocent victims but we had to heed the warning that the rebels could still be lurking in that town. As we crossed the checkpoint I saw Father's body sag and even though I knew he was a strong, proud man I also knew he was human and therefore had a limit.

I offered to assist with the driving to enable him to rest and he did not argue but we were faced with a predicament - Father did not want either one of us to have to get out of the car. I had a strategy that solved the problem confronting us. When Father stopped the car I climbed over to the back seat so he could slide over to the front passenger seat then I climbed into the driver's seat. I recognized that Father was going to be fine when he giggled and exclaimed: "Sister, you so skinny and agile like a monkey, you could fit anywhere!" I was happy to see him relax that I refrained from letting out the hot remark that burned my tongue.

I drove at a casual pace and put on a gospel tape to play when I saw Father's head lolling from side to side indicating that he was asleep. I called out to Frances and she too was asleep so I had no one to converse with. I drove through Tappita, the next large town as well as several other small villages but the image of those dead bodies continually danced before my eyes. My back ached and so did my head and my eyes filled up with tears blurring my vision. Out of nowhere came this chicken and ran straight across the road. I caught sight of it out of the corner of my eye and suddenly swerved the wheel to avoid hitting it.

I had swerved too hard and the car hit an embankment at the side of the road and came to an abrupt halt. Father woke with a jolt and cried out angrily: "Sister! What? You want to kill us all?" When I tried to explain that I didn't want to hit the chicken he vociferously demanded if I preferred to kill three humans instead! That did it for me. I began to tremble with anger and hastily retreated to the back seat declaring that he should continue to drive. Even though he calmed down and apologized I refused to budge so having no choice he got back behind the wheel and continued the journey until we were in Greenville.

As we entered Greenville city hordes of people were gathered on the street and they began to applaud, jump up and down and shout estactically. A happy confusion reigned and I could sense Father's bewilderment. He stopped the car in front of a shop in Pool River and inquired what was wrong. One woman reached through the window and hugged him exclaiming: "Eh Fadda, we so glad to see you, we thought you was dead!" To which Father laughed and responded: "Aha! Radio 'dey say', right?"

The woman shook her head and declared that rumor (radio 'dey say') had it that we were ambushed by the rebels and all killed. I knew that if the sisters had heard that rumor they would be worried sick so I was anxious to get to the convent and assure them that I was very much alive and fine. When I finally got there I just wanted to crawl under my blanket, close my eyes and obliterate the vivid memory of the carnage I had earlier witnessed. No one knew for sure where the rebels were at that point so it was only a matter of time before they attacked again.

CHAPTER EIGHT

School resumed once again and Sister Doris, the Fathers, and I made every effort to keep spirits up and to maintain a sense of normalcy despite the unfavorable news seeping out of Monrovia. Aware of how quickly rumors surfaced and spread like wildfire, we did not know what to believe. We heard that the rebels had penetrated and held Monrovia under siege, that they had captured President Doe, shooting and killing many of his cohorts as well as innocent civilians in the process. Several parents began to be concerned and sought to remove their children from school, but Father Kwesi assured them that these rumors were untrue and that we were not in any danger.

Then, at the beginning of July, Bishop Henry informed us over the CB radio that a crate with our luggage had arrived at the port in Cape Palmas. He had cleared it and it was being stored in his garage. We asked why it was taken all the way to Cape Palmas and he said that the crate had been placed in a container belonging to another missionary group that resided in the Cape, so that's where it went. Sister Doris and I began making plans to drive our station wagon to the Cape to collect our various boxes and suitcases, but Father Kwesi took the matter in hand.

He admonished us for wanting to be so independent and said that we would never survive that harsh journey alone. He and Sister Doris came to loggerheads over this, for she took offense at his implication that we were incapable of doing things for ourselves. Having traveled the inner roads of the country I tended to agree with Father, but still, it would have been an adventure to be all on our own. I advised her not to cross him since he had assumed the role of our guardian angel. If he wanted to help, we should let him because, after all, he was returning home at the end of July so it might be his last good deed as our pastor.

We left Friday afternoon with the hope of returning by Sunday and school on Monday. We arrived in Harper at 3:00 A.M. and when I knocked on the door of the house where Beth and Carol, the lay missionaries, lived, I was welcomed with warm, open arms. Instead of disturbing Bishop Henry at that ungodly hour, Father Kwesi decided to seek lodging at the parish rectory which was directly opposite the house where I was to stay. After snatching a few hours sleep, we were up for 7:00 A.M. Mass at which Father assisted, then we headed over to the bishop's manse which was a ten-minute drive from the church.

I was eager to claim our stuff and be on our way back to Greenville but I had to wait while Bishop Henry had a leisurely breakfast and talked business. He was concerned about the political state of the country. Scores of soldiers had run away from Monrovia and entered Harper from the Ivory Coast through the Cavalla River which separated the countries. They had imposed themselves in that city and were fast infiltrating surrounding village and towns, harassing civilians, stealing their vehicles, livestock, foodstuff and even the wives and girlfriends of the local men.

Bishop Henry had recently acquired a fleet of new vehicles for the diocese and he was worried about the soldiers stealing them. He had obtained permission from the bishop on the Ivory Coast to park the vehicles on the mission there, but Bishop Henry needed courageous men to drive the trucks, vans, and cars onto the ferry and then to the rectory in San Pedro. Father Kwesi was fearless and the bishop immediately enlisted him to assist with that task. After the bishop had breakfasted, he removed the bunch of garage keys from its hiding place and walked over to open and remove the many locks and bolts that secured the double doors.

The top of the crate was removed, and after I inspected the boxes and found everything intact, the bishop told his men to stack the goods onto the decrepit old, white truck parked next to the shiny blue, brand new Bedford in the garage. I saw Father Kwesi's eyebrow arched in silent question. The bishop had also noticed and said defensively: "No ma man, they goin' take that from you if you put it on the road, it goin' over the river!" Father was disappointed but realized that the bishop was right. After the last box was stacked and the whole tray was covered over with tarpaulin, Bishop Henry negotiated with Father to assist driving the vehicles over to the coast. I saw Father's eyes gleam and a wide grin spread over his face. I knew exactly what he was thinking - at least he would get to drive the new truck and some of the other new vehicles too!

To ensure Father's return the bishop made him leave his car in Harper and ride on the truck. The bishop sent his own trusted driver, Sam, who apparently had amassed years of experience traveling the length and breadth of the country. He boasted that Sam was just the one to deal with those rascal soldiers should we encounter them and they give us hell. We left Harper after lunch and I had hoped to see Sam put to the test, but surprisingly we arrived in Greenville in the wee hours of the morning having had no rough encounters with the soldiers. Since it was so late and we had none of the boys to help, Father suggested that they drop me off and return the next day with plenty of help to unload the boxes. This was done around seven o'clock the next morning because Father hoped to leave right after Mass which was at nine o'clock.

Each day brought another group of soldiers to Greenville and they wasted no time in revealing their vile, cruel, thieving, wanton ways. They harassed the shopkeepers and emptied the shelves of the shops. They made civilian drivers halt in the middle of the streets, hauled them out of their vehicles, threw them on the dirt road, and rode off in the stolen cars, trucks, jeeps, and even bicycles. Women flocked to these dirty, unkempt creatures and followed them like bees. A group of them found their way on the mission that Sunday and proceeded to create havoc. They wanted the truck, but when Sam saw them coming he quickly removed a part from the engine. Without it the truck would not start, and when the soldiers realized it, they left without it.

This however deferred the journey by a day. Father realized that to travel in daylight would be disastrous, so they planned to leave in the dark of night. Everyone warned him and Sam to be extremely cautious and I advised that if the soldiers accosted them for the rotten old truck they should give it up without a fight. I knew it would go against Father's grain since he felt that he had to prove that he was bigger and stronger than everyone else, but I said, "For peace's sake, be humble this once so you will return alive!" I also pleaded with him to radio the port office and inform us that they had arrived safely or if anything went amiss.

When I arrived at school that Monday morning it felt strange not having Father Kwesi there to welcome us. It was the first time that I had not traveled with him and I felt angry and sad. It was not yet a full year since we had arrived, and I had become good friends with both priests, but especially with Father Kwesi to whom I had grown extremely close despite his rough, harsh manner. He reminded me so much of Sister Emma.

I could read him like the back of my hand now. He was a big coward with sensitive feelings and a heart of gold despite his immense size, gruff manner, and big mouth. He had an insatiable appetite for life and transmitted this enthusiasm to those around him. He delighted in speaking in parables, whether he was on the pulpit or conversing casually. He loved playing card games, listening to music, drinking beer, and doing justice to a well-cooked meal. He delighted in telling stories and making people laugh, but he also had a quiet, serious side that made people flock to him. A sense of justice and a deep wisdom characterized this man of God and made him the Solomon of the Catholic mission. People knocked on his door at any time of the day or night to help them make decisions.

Since we worked closely together, Father learned that I had one aim -- the welfare of my students and their families. He had become very fond and rather possessive of me. Yet we formed a good team, we were constantly at loggerheads. I spoke my mind freely about situations I didn't like and he felt that I was too bold and self-sufficient for so young a woman. He challenged my wisdom, my methods of teaching, my efforts to create a better environment for my students, and almost broke my spirit a few times. But I strengthened my resolve and, as he revealed one day, when he saw that I was made of leather, not plastic, he learned to trust and accept me.

I was able to converse with this giant of a man about any and every subject. To me he revealed his darkest fears, secrets, and shortcomings, while I in turn opened myself one inch at a time to him because I was still cautious about growing close to anyone since Sister Emma had passed away. He was weak where women were concerned. When I saw women closing in and sensed he would be hurt I cautioned him both gently and harshly, to make him listen.

Little did I know that Father was protecting me silently in the same way. One day when we were speaking open-heartedly, he revealed that he was doing battle keeping the men away from me. I had not been aware of this, and he said that was because he kept them so far away from me. African men go to great lengths to prove their sexual prowess. They live to conquer women and believe no woman can resist their charms and efforts to win them over. Even though I was a foreigner and a religious sister, I was no exception. Father revealed that several men had approached him and even offered him money to have me. I was shocked and angry at this revelation. And to think I was so naïve; not for one minute did I suspect anything, but then it dawned on me why Father was so possessive of me. He made himself felt when we went anywhere and men approached me. On the school campus, if the male teachers or fathers of students wanted to speak to me in private, he always remained close. My anger soon turned to a deep sense of gratitude. I felt greatly loved and protected, which reminded me of the way I felt when

I was a child in the presence of my father.

Despite his outer harshness I had touched a tender spot that was sometimes revealed when Father was dealing with the students. I cared for my students with a fierce compassion and desire to see them achieve their very best. Sometimes when I pushed them too hard, Father would admonish, "You young, Sister. With all your learning and college degree, you don't know these people as I do!" I didn't understand at first because he knew that I wanted only the best for these young men and women, but it was as if he felt that I was trying to steal them from him or exceed his efforts. I suspected that he was scared and reluctant to depart from the school and the parish, and I understood his vulnerability. Never had I seen him so human.

One morning we had an exceptionally hot altercation. He wanted to flog a student who was late for school. Father Kwesi flogged the students - male and female - unmercifully. I was horrified when I first witnessed him doing it and I vowed to abolish that practice. Oh, I did believe in punishing negative behavior, but I never resorted to corporal punishment. As he raised the rod to strike Christian that morning, I crept up behind him, grabbed his arm, pulled away the rod, and yelled to the boy to run. Father was angry and just for one minute I thought he was going to strike me, but he didn't.

I stormed out of his office in search of Christian who had gone back to his tenth grade homeroom. I was about to teach the tenth grade class religion and I knew Christian loved this class. He always paid keen attention and asked a lot of questions which generated lively discussion. Christian had a deep desire to become a priest, and this class fed his quest for knowledge of the religion. I gently but firmly told Christian to go and take a swiper from the cupboard and cut the grass in front of the church. I saw the hurt and disappointed look in his eyes and I knew I had accomplished what Father would not have had he flogged Christian. That was how I was trained to punish - by depriving persons of something they loved or valued while they did something useful.

I had classes all morning so I didn't see Father Kwesi. At 2:00 P.M. after the bell was rung to dismiss the school for the day, I was returning to my office when I saw Christian coming out of Father Kwesi's office. As I approached the door to my office, Christian stopped me and asked if he could speak to me. He apologized for being late explaining that he had chores to perform at home before coming to school. He also thanked me for "saving his butt," as he put it but he said it hurt him more to have missed my class, so he had learned his lesson. After he left, I was so engrossed in preparing my class for the evening school that I did not see Father Kwesi standing in my doorway.

I did not know how long he had stood there, but when I realized it, I invited him to come in and sit. Before he did, he apologized to me. Father Kwesi apologizing? Well, I had certainly accomplish what others thought was impossible! But I did not gloat because I knew he was hurting, I could tell by the tone of his voice, the sad look in his eyes, and the droop of his shoulders. "You don't really want to leave this place and return to Ghana, do you Father?" I asked. "Oh Sister, you know me like you know your prayer manual!" He said sadly. "I thought I had everything under control, and even though I have grown to love this place and the people during the past six years, I thought walking away would be easy, but it isn't. And to add to my pain you walk in, young, beautiful, and all the people fall at your feet and fly to do your bidding like if I was gone already. For the first time in my life, Sister, I don't have matters under control. I don't have all the answers and I can't cope!"

My heart went out to him and there and then I silently pledged to make him feel as wanted and appreciated as possible until his departure. I gently assured him that I had no intentions of "stealing" the people from him or pushing him aside because I depended on him for guidance and support in finding my way around the school and parish. I consoled him and revealed that I was just as impassioned about my work there as he was. He said he did not doubt that, as he had seen from the very beginning I wanted nothing but the best for and from my students.

Father Kwesi looked at me fondly and sounded so much like my father when he said: "Fine girl, Father Kofi and I feel like you're one of us. You treat us like gentlemen, with respect and acceptance. You don't criticize or make us feel unintelligent and inferior like the others do. Even though your ideas are different and modern, you always consult us first not go ahead and do what you want like the others do." By now I had inferred that by'others he meant the other Sisters but I didn't ask. I was touched deeply when they realized that I cared a great deal for them, for the mission, and especially for my students. Father confessed that I had accomplished at the mission what none of the other sisters had.

That Monday morning in July 1990 I sat in my office and missed Father Kwesi dreadfully. I said a silent prayer that he would be protected and arrive at his destination safely. Just as I finished my prayer there was a knock on the door and when I answered it was Father Kofi. Even though he lived in Father Kwesi's shadow I had also formed a deep friendship with him. He was very shy and uninformed about many subjects. We journeyed weekly to the three outstations, distributed holy communion to the aged and bedridden members of the St. Joseph's parish and did other chores together, I was able to penetrate his quiet reserve and delighted in teaching him about the bigger world, the world outside of Africa about which he had very little knowledge.

As Father Kofi stood in my office, he declared that he was having unpleasant feelings about Father Kwesi's trip. I confided to him the anxiety I was feeling as well, and we just looked at each other helplessly. Then while neither of us felt we could do anything, we knew the good Lord would, we decided to implore his help. After voicing our despair to God, we resolutely left everything up to him. Having found temporary relief from our concern about the safety of our shepherd, Father Kwesi, we made every effort to maintain as normal a composure so the students would not suspect our distress.

At midday Father Kofi sent one of the students to call me to join him for lunch. The cook had prepared palm butter and rice, which had become my favorite Liberian meal and the fathers knew it. Just as we sat down and began our meal we heard a car draw up outside the house. We both ran out and saw Ray, an elder of the church and the port manager, approaching. From the grim look on his face I knew he did not come bearing good news.

He quickly explained the reason for his visit. Father had called him from one of the logging companies just off the border of Sinoe County. He, Sam and the numerous passengers they had picked up along the way were all unharmed and in relatively good spirits but "Betsy," Sam's beloved truck was gone. They had been ambushed by a group of government soldiers led by someone called Apollo Jayswah, a terrorist whom everyone despised and feared. He and his cohorts dealt roughly with Sam and demanded that he and his passengers get out and hand the truck over to him.

This had taken place in the middle of nowhere, and Father was certain they would all be killed by this pack of villains who had no respect for the uniform they wore nor for the lives they were supposed to protect. Father advised Sam to hand over the keys without a fight so that their lives would be spared. Sam obeyed Father and they stood helplessly while Apollo drove off with Betsy. When they were sure it was safe they began to walk back to a village they had passed through some ten miles back. In this village was a Methodist mission, and to Father's relief and delight, the missionaries had a short wave radio. He called the port and relayed their dilemma.

Ray assured us that they were all fine and wanted our permission to take the sisters' station wagon to go and bring them back to Greenville. We of course agreed, and soon Ray was on his way to the camp to retrieve Father and his traveling companions. He returned just after nightfall and came directly to the convent. We were relieved to see that everyone was well and unharmed, but Father Kwesi was seething with anger. He swore that the last thing he would do before returning to Ghana was to recover the truck from Apollo. Sisters Angela and Doris tried to reason with him, but I saw the mood he was in and knew he wouldn't listen to anyone.

Father had a few of his friends secretly search out the whereabouts of Apollo and the truck, and soon learned that the truck was kept in the main camp of the soldiers in Zwedru. Father began making arrangements to journey to Zwedru. In the meantime, he and Sam would travel to Harper the next day with Simon, one of the parishioners, to return with the fathers' car. Simon was from Sierra Leone and both he and his wife were vibrant members of the church community. When the government soldiers infiltrated Greenville, they attacked Simon and his family, stealing most of their belongings and a large sum of money. Simon feared for the safety of his family so all he wished to do was to return to his homeland. Very sadly the next day, all the parishioners gathered outside the church to bid farewell to Simon and his family and to wish Father Kwesi and Sam a safe return to Greenville.

True to his word, Father returned to Greenville on Thursday, which meant that Father Kofi would be able to go out to the outstations that Sunday. Father and I were accompanied by John, an elder of the church, Andrew, the parish catechist, and Joan, his girlfriend. We drove to the furthest outstation, Juarzon, first. This village was about forty-five miles from Greenville and was a new outstation. There were only a handful of Catholics, but many desired to be converted to the faith. We usually held services in the elementary school, but the elders had recently offered us ten acres of land on which to construct a church and a high school.

A young man, Anthony, served as catechist in that village. He was originally from Greenville and was instrumental in influencing the elders of the village to give us the land on which to build. He was a sincere, amiable young man who was very dedicated to his work among the people in that village. After Mass that Sunday, he guided Father and our team to a few homes where there were sick people. Father prayed with and consoled them. The last home we entered was the home of the oldest elder of the village. He could not speak a work of English, but through Anthony, who served as interpreter, he thanked Father and our team, then said something which made Anthony smile broadly and look at me shyly. When I asked what the old man had said, he revealed that this old man, who already had five wives and had fathered over twenty children, wished that I would stay and marry him. I laughed and replied that I would think about his proposition.

Our next stop was a village that wasn't rural in any way. You could have easily imagined yourself in the heart of Monrovia, the capital of the country. It was nestled within a camp that housed the workers of the country's only palm oil company and their families. I was impressed when I first visited that community. It was built and maintained by the Korean company that managed the factory. The houses were of concrete, built and maintained by the foreigners. There was a first-class hospital, a modern, up-to-date school, and electricity and running water were available to all. Many of the students in Greenville had friends and relatives in that community and could not wait for school to be out so that they could spend their vacation there.

An active Catholic community among the villagers was led by a smiling, exuberant Mike, the catechist. Mike was a real city guy, which was emphasized by the flaming red motorcycle he rode. He kept the faith burning and the spirit alive among the faithful in the absence of the priests and the sisters who went every week to teach catechism classes. The number of converts was close to one hundred, which included children and adults, but this number grew constantly. A group close to forty waited for Sister Doris to prepare them for their First Communion and almost twice that number were ready to receive Confirmation classes, which I would teach. There was also an exceptional choir led by Mike's brother, Garth, who also played the guitar and drums.

When our team arrived that Sunday, we found a large gathering awaiting us for Mass, which was usually held in the junior school. Immediately I entered the room I could sense a difference in their demeanor and spirit. I looked around and saw nervous and scared faces. I removed Father Kofi's gown from his traveling case, shook it out to remove wrinkles, and as I handed it to him I whispered, "Father, something's amiss; the people don't seem their normal selves!" Father said that I was only imagining things, that maybe they were still sleepy. I was not convinced, but I refrained from saying anything further.

As Mass progressed, the choir lacked its usual lustiness, and the elders seemed less cheerful and chatty. Everyone seemed restless and nervous. After Mass, everyone hastened to their homes instead of staying around to socialize as they always did. I was convinced that something was wrong. I called Mike aside and asked if everything was okay. He glanced around furtively then took hold of my arm and pulled me closer to him. In a barely audible voice and eyes wide with terror, Mike revealed the reason for their distress.

There was a beautiful beach just outside the borders of the camp in an area called Baffle Bay. This linked Monrovia and the northern region of the country to the southern area which was where we were. Two men who had gone there before daybreak to fish had returned with the report that the rebel gang who had attacked Monrovia had been seen walking along the beach and among the bushes surrounding the bay. One of the men was a brother of Mike and the other was a family friend and since the men had not actually seen the rebels themselves, they had said nothing in public realizing that they could cause panic over a simple rumor.

I looked around to find Father Kofi and when I saw him, I

motioned for him to come to where I stood with Mike. As he strode in our direction I noticed two other men accompanying him and realized that we couldn't say anything in front of them. I had to think fast, and when the three men stood before us, I looked at Mike and raised my eyebrow and then said to Father, "Father, Mike wants you to hear his confession but was reluctant to ask because he thought you may not have the time."

As I was saying this I took Father's hand and put it in Mike's so Mike could lead him away to a quiet spot. Confession is one of the sacraments of the church and a very private matter between the priest and the penitent. Therefore the two men didn't dare follow Father. I chatted a few minutes with them, then eased my way out of the building in search of Mike and Father. I soon espied them in another classroom, entered it and shut the door. I was in time to hear Father reassuring Mike because he was sure the story was only an unfounded rumor. I asked Mike if there was any place they could run away to hide if there was an attack, and he replied that most of the people in the camp were from Monrovia or some other country and so were unfamiliar with the forest. If the rebels were to enter the area through the forest, the civilians did not stand a chance.

Whenever Father Kofi and I went out to the nearby villages we always shared the driving and that day it was my turn to drive us back to Greenville. I could feel the fear and nervousness welling up in my stomach but I did not want to alert or scare the others. So I set out at a leisurely pace and even struck up a lively conversation with Andrew and the others in the back seat.

We had entered a dense, lonely stretch of forest area when suddenly I thought I heard a gunshot. My throat grew dry and my hands were like blocks of ice. I averted my eyes from the road for a few seconds when I heard Father Kofi scream, "Look out for that rock in the road, Sister!" I turned my head and saw the car was heading straight toward a huge rock in the middle of the road. I swiftly twisted the wheel but angled it too much, and the car landed in a ditch on the side of the road.

For a moment the only sound filling my ears was the wild pounding of my heart. Then I became aware of a clacking sound and realized that I was so nervous my knees were knocking. I soon recovered and asked if the others were okay. They said were unharmed. Father asked if I was fit to continue driving and I replied that I was. I pulled the car out of the dirt mound and guided it back on to the dirt road heading to Greenville City. Our journey continued without incident and we arrived in Greenville about an hour later. No one mentioned this accident and we did not hear any more talk of rebels nor did they appear.

When I had begun teaching English in the high school I had discovered that many of the students had great writing skills, and I was always seeking ways to channel that talent. One of the Peace Corps workers with whom I was friendly often gave me a copy of their monthly newsletter to read. All the Peace Corps workers who served in the country contributed stories or articles about their work or other subjects. I found this newsletter stimulating and interesting, but it also gave me a brilliant idea. I would introduce the idea of a school magazine to the students.

In addition to being principal of the high school I was class mistress of the eleventh grade. There were twenty-two students in this class, and when I suggested that they organize the magazine, they were elated. The students decided that I should be the editor while Matthew, a transfer student from Zwedru, was chosen as the assistant editor. He was an A student with an excellent command of both written and spoken English. Myra, another transfer student from Zwedru, was elected Treasurer, and the remaining students were divided up into reporters and a production team.

One of the students, Joel, who excelled in art, was to design a cover. He had become very vocal in advocating peace in light of the unstable situation embroiling the country. It was not surprising when he came into my office and proudly presented an accurate and exquisite drawing of a dove under the wording "THE DOVE" written in fancy writing. I congratulated Joel, and when I showed it to the class, everyone agreed that it was a fitting name for our magazine. The production team set about making posters, inviting everyone to submit poems, stories, pieces of humor, etc. while the special reporters went about gathering information for their articles.

As a fitting tribute, the first edition was to be dedicated to Father Kwesi, so contributors were encouraged to dedicate their writings to him. One reporter was to do an interview of Father, and when the final article was submitted the students and I gathered in the classroom to read, screen, and ultimately select the ones for publication. As many as twenty typewriters had been amassed by the sisters before us, to teach the students to type. I searched around the convent and junior school and was able to find five and with these the few students who could type began preparing the stencil templates. There was a beat-up, outdated, manual Gestetner printing machine in the school, and as one crew typed, I taught another to set the stencils and print them.

We experienced many frustrations as we worked the machine. It kept spewing out the ink, and pretty soon Arthur, who was turning the spindle, was covered in the sticky black liquid. There was also a gross waste of precious paper. Then, in an effort to keep this whole operation as a surprise to Father, we had to keep the classroom locked, but he kept sneaking up, attempting to spy on us. So we had one student as a "lookout" to alert us when Father approached.

After much trial and tribulation, the machine began to work well and turned out clean, clear almost perfect pages. The students were elated, jumping around hugging each other. I had to remind them that the pages still had to be put in order and stapled. There was an audible groan, but they settled down and resumed production.

As dark began to descend we surveyed our handiwork. On the last desk was stacked one hundred copies of our school magazine, _The Dove_. We chose the three best copies, rolled them individually, and tied each one with some green ribbon. These were to be presented during assembly the next morning to Father Kwesi, Father Kofi, and Sister Doris. The rest of the copies were to be sold at one dollar a copy. My students were so proud of themselves.

Back home when I worked with my youth groups, after occasions like this one, I would normally take them for pizza or ice-cream, but there was not that luxury in Greenville, so I had to be content with congratulating and thanking them. I urged them to have confidence in themselves without becoming arrogant. I said this proved that they could achieve any task they set their minds to. I encouraged them to pursue their dreams with constancy and dedication.

The day after the presentations was Friday, July 26th, and it was a grand holiday to celebrate the independence of the country. Father Kwesi had made plans to go to Zwedru that day to reclaim the truck from the soldier who had stolen it. Originally, it was agreed that Father Kofi and I would accompany him, but that Thursday evening after Mass, Father nonchalantly declared to father Kofi and me, "I think you should both stay back, yah. I will take Simon [the mission boy], John [the mechanic], and two other parishioners. Don't worry we will we fine."

Needless to say, Father Kofi and I were disappointed and a bit concerned, but it was so characteristic of him - impetuous and practical. And, there was no use arguing. We ourselves had to journey into town to purchase bread and other commodities, and we encountered many groups of drunk, unruly soldiers.

Near the first shop, the leader of one group approached us and demanded we give him the car. Sister Doris was driving and firmly stated that we couldn't do that because we lived a long way from town. A scowl crossed the soldier's face, and she offered to give them a lift to wherever they were going. He gave her a long hard look and with an angry wave of his hand dismissed us as he spat out one word: "Go!" Sister guided the car through the nearest side road and we swiftly left the area and headed for the convent, forgetting about our bread for supper as well as the other things we needed.

Since the sisters had no special plans for the Independence holiday, I decided to go and work in the school. I left right after breakfast hoping to say good-bye to Father Kwesi and his travelers but by the time I got to the campus they were already gone. My heart sank to my feet and I got a weird sensation in the pit of my stomach, so I headed to my office and buried my head in work. I had posters to make for my classes and assignments to mark, but my mind wasn't really there. Around midmorning, Father Kofi came and asked to borrow the car to go and shop for meat and vegetables.

I was in the depth of preparing lesson plans when I heard a car speed up into the school yard and stop abruptly in front of my office. As I rushed out, Father Kofi rushed in the front door shouting, "Sister, Sister, lock up the office and go home! Quick, the rebels are coming!" I hurried out in time to see truckloads of the government soldiers who had sought refuge in Greenville, as well as police officers by the carloads racing along the road in front of the school campus. This road led away from Greenville City and out of Sinoe County so I realized that these officers of the law were running away from something or someone.

Father was terrorstruck but I calmed him enough to tell me what was wrong. He said that he had been heading to a farming area called Plantesite, but was swiftly turned back. Plantesite was about thirty miles from B.O.P.C., the camp where we had an outstation and where the villagers were rumored to have seen the rebels entering through the forest and beach. The villagers of Plantesite were all running off to the forest or other areas, because they claimed that the rebels were in B.O.P.C. and fast advancing to nearby villages. They strongly advised Father to return to Greenville and warn the people there. I became frozen with fear as Father Kofi repeated several times, "What are we going to do, Sister, what are we going to do?"

I quickly locked up my office and moved woodenly toward the car. Father felt that I shouldn't go alone, so he decided to accompany me to a distance that was safe enough to proceed on my own. As we drove along the road, civilians, young and old, were already fleeing in a frenzy to reach the forest before the rebels arrived and attacked the town. The police station was along the route we took and not one officer was in sight. When I turned into the Farmersville road, which was deserted, Father suggested that I let him off and he would walk back to the mission through a sidetrack that was well hidden from the main road. I was reluctant, but he assured me that he would be careful, so I did as he asked and drove off, anxious to get to the convent and alert the sisters.

When I got to the house all appeared to be normal. Ben and his two young helpers, Martin and Oliver, were filling up the water barrels. I did not want to alarm them so I called the sisters into my bedroom and closed the door. Although I was shaking with fear I calmly related what was happening out in the town. Sisters Angela and Doris were alarmed but also remained calm. We decided not to scare Ben or the boys, but after about thirty minutes, all the villagers around the convent began to run off.

Ben, who was in the yard hanging out the washing, called out in Kru and asked what was happening. One word: "Rebels!" was enough to make Ben's eyes pop in terror. At the same time Martin and Oliver who were attending the grass around the clinic came running toward the house. They began to shout that the rebels were coming and they wanted to go to their families. We sent the three men home warning them to be careful. When they left I walked around the house, sensing the desolation and emptiness, and smelling the fear in the air.

We tried to continue a normal routine. We prayed our Midday Prayer, had lunch, and then retired to our rooms. I decided to take a nap and was just dozing off when I was awakened by a loud boom. Surely that could not have been a gunshot? I sped out of my room and was joined by the other two sisters in the corridor. Suddenly the world around us seemed to be exploding. Shots rang out from what sounded like every direction. Sister Doris, who had previously experienced war, shouted at us to "hit the floor," lie flat, and stay there. We lay on the floor for what seemed like hours but the shooting never ceased. It had faded somewhat, which indicated that the rebels had entered the city. We had no idea what was happening and could only wait and hope that someone had escaped and would bring us news, but the waiting was hell.

When the firing seemed very distant, we thought it was safe to get up off the floor but we moved around the house cautiously. The hours crept by agonizingly until it was time to get on the radio and communicate with the other missionaries. The three of us crouched around the table where the radio sat and spoke in very hushed tones. In coded messages we informed the bishop that we had "visitors" and Father Kofi also told him that Father Kwesi had left that morning heading for Zwedru to retrieve the truck that had been taken from him. Bishop Henry exploded in anger. "I told Kwesi to leave the rotten old truck alone! Eh yah, but why the man so stubborn and hard headed?"

Father Kofi's statement suddenly hit me - if Father had encountered those rebels, what fate had he suffered? I was suddenly overcome with fear. I clutched my stomach and cried out: "Oh God!" then retreated to my room. I heard Father Kofi's voice over the radio informing everyone that he was fine and would come by the convent the next day.

None of us slept that night but kept vigil in either the chapel or our rooms. As Saturday's dawn slowly broke, I turned on my transistor radio to listen to the BBC news. Astonishment and shock clouded my mind as I listened to the first news item. There had been a coup in my own home country. Sister Doris had also heard the report and came rushing out of her room just as I rushed out of mine to report what I had heard. That was a double blow for me. There I was in the middle of a war and coincidentally having to worry about the safety of my family, thousands of miles away, facing the same plight! My one thought was - it couldn't get worse!

Around midmorning, Father Kofi and Dennis, one of the parishioners, came to the convent to bring us some fresh meat and bread. Then they told us a most incredible story. Simon, the mission boy, had returned to the mission around midnight. He was bleeding from several gunshot wounds and extremely weak, having walked almost ten miles. All three sisters asked in unison, "But what of Father Kwesi and the others?" Father Kofi looked at us with the saddest expression in his eyes, put his head in his hands, and burst into tears. We knew then that the worst had happened, but I wasn't ready to accept the worst so easily. Dennis continued relaying Simon's story.

Father was driving at his usual reckless speed, the car stereo blaring, and was approaching a town called Butaw, about ten miles from B.O.P.C., when the car was suddenly sprayed with bullets. The car came to an abrupt stop and the rebels surrounded it and ordered everyone out. As the three men in the back seat stepped out, they realized that they had all been shot, and when they called out to Father he was unconscious. One soldier wrenched open the door, and as Father fell out sideways, the rebel kicked him and rolled him over. Father, barely conscious, pleaded with the soldier: "I am a priest, and these are my church people, please let us go." The rebel had his gun pointed at Father and kept shouting: "Damn Krahn man!"

Father was mistaken for a member of the Krahn tribe, and when Father asked Simon to get his passport and license book out of his pocket and give it to the rebel, he did so but the heartless, cruel rebel grabbed the documents from Simon's hand and threw them into the bushes, then began to pump bullets into Father as he lay on the ground. The three men ran quickly into the nearby bushes, but Simon stayed by Father's side as the rebels left even though he had been shot in his leg, back, and buttocks. Sister Doris held her mouth in horror as Father Kofi took over from Dennis.

According to Simon, Father was moaning and bleeding to death and all he could do was comfort Father as best he could.

After a few hours Simon heard vehicles approaching and dragging himself out into the open flagged down the first jeep that was whizzing past. He courageously faced the various guns aimed at him and begged the rebels to help get medical assistance for Father. Simon recognized the young man who stepped down and told him to lead him to where Father Kwesi lay.

Ironically, that young man's family were prominent members of the Catholic parish in Greenville, and he even had brothers in the school. He recognized Father and promised Simon that he would take him to the hospital in B.O.P.C. The rebel, Warren, ordered one of the other drivers to take Simon to town whilst he returned to the hospital with Father in his vehicle. And that was the last Simon saw of Father. When the rebels had driven a short distance they ordered Simon, shot and bleeding, to get out and walk the rest of the way into town.

Shortly before midnight Father Kofi heard a pounding on his front door. He went to answer not knowing who or what to expect. Opening the door he saw no one, but peering closely into the darkness, he made out the form of a body on the ground. Father awoke Robert and two other boys who were sleeping in the mission house. They brought lanterns and looked at the figure but could not identify it because the person was covered in dirt and blood. Then they heard a weak whisper, "Father Kofi, is me, Simon." After washing his body and feeding him, they realized that Simon was badly hurt and had to get attention immediately. With the help of the other two boys Robert lifted Simon into the canoe and took him across the river to a medicine man who resided in a village on the other side of the river.

Father tried to reassure us that Father Kwesi would be all right and Sister Angela reiterated his assurance. Dennis then brought us up-to-date with what was happening in town. The rebels had invaded and taken over homes while they sought out members of the Kru tribe. Numerous individuals were killed as they crossed the path of the rebels when entering the city. One Guinean truck driver who lived near the church was killed as he drove a logging truck out of the city. One of the senior students of the high school ran out into the street as the rebels approached and was instantly cut down with a blow to his neck with a cutlass. And so the list of dead grew.

The group of rebels that had entered Greenville City was part of the NPFL (National Patriotic Front of Liberia) founded by Charles Harper, whose aim was to overthrow President Samuel Doe and become the next leader of Liberia. But it soon escalated into a full-scale civil war when the struggle became a tribal issue with the massacre of different groups or tribes depending on the area and the tribes dwelling there. The soldiers called themselves the "Freedom Fighters" because they said they were saving Liberians from the tyranny and oppression of the present regime.

It was reported that those who entered and attacked the county of Sinoe had done so to save members of the Kru tribe, supposedly killed off by the Saapo tribe. As a result, when the rebels arrived, they plundered and massacred members of the Saapo tribe. Juarzon, an extensively populated Saapo area where we had our second outstation, was burned to the ground and most of the villagers, including our catechist, were murdered. Those who managed to escape into the forest were hunted down like animals; others were harassed by the rebels, who took away all their belongings, stripped their farms, as they mercilessly plundered their way through the village.

The same fate was suffered by villages all along the way from Juarzon to Greenville City. Civilians who were caught by the rebels were tied in a most cruel way. The locals referred to it as being "tabayed" by the rebels. The civilians' arms were pulled back as tightly as possible and wrapped around the person's back then they were tied at the elbows. This cut off their ability to breathe normally. The captured civilian was then stripped down to their underwear and paraded up and down the streets of the town. Their final fate was a severe beating which led to their being shot, chopped or kicked to death. At first, only members of the offending tribe were subjected to this treatment but the rebels became so wild that they began to capture persons at random and torture them in that same manner.

Father Kofi and Dennis continued relating their tale of horror, but I was past listening. I was blinded and deafened by an overpowering sense of anger and fear. The passionate caregiver in me wanted to hide and protect all those for whom I had come to care deeply, especially my students. I felt desperately helpless and this made me angry and terrified. Father warned us to stay out of sight and just hope and pray that the soldiers didn't come to the convent. Dennis added that if they did come and demand something we should not argue or resist. I found that hard to swallow. It wasn't that I could not obey but I was not about to hand over my life to those cruel, senseless ruffians.

The next day, Sunday, July 28, Father Kofi and Dennis came by to take the station wagon and go in search of Father Kwesi. They had to obtain special permission from Noreiga, the rebel leader and would be escorted by rebel guards. Their escort would be Warren, the rebel whom Simon had identified as the one who offered to seek medical assistance for Father. Some members of the Ghanaian community also accompanied Father Kofi and Dennis. They went to perform certain rituals on the corpse in the event Father Kwesi was dead. Sister Doris made every effort to be cheerful and suggested that we prepare one of the guest rooms where we would keep Father and nurse him back to health, so we busied ourselves doing just that.

It was just after midday when we heard Father Kofi drive up in front of the convent. We ran out to greet him and found a desolate, heartbroken man who was making every effort to be strong. He didn't look at any of us but said in an emotion-filled voice, barely over a whisper, "We brought him back and the funeral is in a half hour. I will be back to pick you up," and with that he drove off. We were too stunned and confused to grasp the full impact of his words. I turned to Sister Doris: "He did say 'funeral,' didn't he? So that meant that somebody is dead, right?

Oh my God, Father Kwesi?" Siister Doris grabbed her stomach and cried out, but I was too shocked to cry. I gathered up the paper flowers I had fashioned from crepe paper to decorate the church for the Mass we were to hold for Father Kwesi's farewell. I didn't have time to make a wreath so I jut tied them in a large bunch to place on the coffin.

Father Kofi returned for us as promised, and as we entered the compound of the mission, we saw people standing, sitting and reposing in every corner of the house and the yard around. Men, women, and children were crying softly, moaning their death cry, pulling at their hair, beating their breasts, and wailing loudly. It seemed as though the whole of Sinoe County was present to mourn Father's death. Intermingled among the crowd of mourners were grim-looking, unkempt young men and boys bearing every size and shape of guns.

After Father Kofi parked the car we hurried off to the church which was jammed-pack with every class and faith of people in the community. Then some soldiers suddenly lined the back of the church and rudely informed Father Kofi that he had ten minutes to be done with his "simi-dimi." I turned around and looked with much hostility at the rebel who had made that comment. Father knew that whatever he said would be censored so he refrained from preaching any sermon. I did the readings for the service, not because I wanted to, but because I was the only dry-eyed person present in the church. Father Kofi could barely contain his grief and simply went through the motions of the ceremony which was finished within the ten minutes allotted. A grave was dug in the far right corner to the front of the church and amidst wailing, moaning, angry shouts, silent tears, and stoicism, Father Kwesi's remains were laid to rest.

After the burial we all retreated to the house where Sister Doris began to pray the rosary. We hadn't completed the "Our Father" prayer when Robert came and whispered to Father Kofi. Father turned to us and quietly said, "Another group of rebels was spotted entering Greenville, and we have been give ten minutes to clear the mission, so we have to get you home fast." We left the car on the mission and Father, along with some parishioners, walked us through a shortcut in the bushes that led directly to the convent. When we were close, they left us and turned around to return to the mission. No sooner were we safely within the walls of the convent than loud gunfire erupted and assaulted our senses once again. We looked at each other and silently prayed that Father Kofi and the others had safely returned.

CHAPTER NINE

The reality of the rebel invasion, the death of Father Kwesi, the dangers we faced by remaining in that territory, coupled with worry for the safety of my own family finally took its toll on me. I began to suffer delayed reaction and react I did. I did not rise for prayer, I hardly ate, and I virtually ceased to exist for the next few days. I locked my door, turned on my radio, and cried buckets of tears. I knew that was how I dealt with grief and I simply had to go through the process. I moved the bed, wardrobe, and desk - all heavy oak furniture, in my room, arranging and rearranging them until every muscle in my body hurt.

On the third day of my depression, I told myself that I had to get a grip on things because we were all alone in that deserted, war-ridden, seemingly godforsaken place, thousands of miles from family and friends. Those with whom I had become friends had either run away into the forest or were dead. I had no idea what I was going to do but I knew I had to snap out of that desolate, despairing frame of mind fast. I took a long, cold bath, dressed in one of the local dresses I usually wore in the house, combed out my waist length hair, which I had not combed in days, and reentered the land of the living. The sisters did not ask any questions or make any comments, and we made every effort to lead as normal a life as we possibly could under the circumstances.

At the end of August Sister Angela decided to open the clinic for a few hours each day because people were beginning to trek up to the convent requesting medical attention. All sister's staff from the clinic had run off into the forest so she operated all alone. Sister Doris and I were stuck in the house since we dared not think about going to the school campus. As the days progressed we discovered new things to occupy our time and keep our minds sane. I manually dug up the entire front yard which had been planted with a thick hard grass known as carpet grass. Once properly groomed it did indeed give the impression of a lush green carpet but it destroyed anything else that was planted in its path and it also harbored snakes.

I molded the earth to form beds and planted various beans and greens which eventually were used for our meals. All the shops in town were closed when the owners ran off but the rebels broke the locks and looted out all the stock that was left there. Our food supply had dwindled considerably so we had to be extra frugal. The three of us were pitifully thin and we took extra precautions not to become malnourished. As more and more patients attended the clinic sister did not turn away anyone even when they claimed they didn't have the dollar to pay the visiting fee. Instead, they began to bring chickens and produce from their farms that had escaped the rebels. In that way we were saved from imminent starvation. Sister Doris and I thrived on the bread baked by the members of the Fanti tribe in a special dirt oven but the joy of having that bread every day was short-lived once the rebels had attacked.

The Fanti tribe was a tribe of Ghanaian people who had set-tled along the coast. They owned fleets of canoes with which they fished each day providing the town with an ample supply of fresh fish and even lobsters, which one could purchase for a mere dollar. They baked bread and they excelled in preparing the "dry bony" which the Liberians (and our dog, Beego) loved so much. Dry bony was prepared by smoking in a special way the herrings that the fishermen caught. Not everyone knew how to prepare the fire for smoking because the Fanti used special wood known only to them.

When Noreiga and his band of notorious thieves entered the city they immediately set upon the Fanti people. Their canoes were seized, their homes were ransacked, their produce stolen, and many of the members killed. Some of the more prominent members of this tribe boasted that they had tons of money and that was what the rebels wanted. It was rumored that they took away hundreds of thousands of dollars. For weeks on end they were randomly rounded up like cattle, robbed, beaten, humiliated in every possible way, and even killed. One day several of them - both men and women - were stripped naked, taken to the beach, and told to "swim" in the sand; then they were executed. Their bodies were buried in shallow graves in the sand but moments later, they were unearthed by dogs who dragged them around the houses of their camp.

Those who survived spent most of the time huddled together in hiding. Father Kofi was extremely angered over the treatment of his people but dared not openly help them. Instead, he begged someone to find somewhere for them to stay. Father then asked me to help, and I seized every opportunity to take them food and medicine. The house where they were was not large enough, and soon became unsafe when the rebels suspected they were there, so one night when the sky was pitch black with neither the moon nor a single star in sight, we transferred them to the mission. There were close to fifty women and children. Those men who had not been killed were advised to run into the forest, but someone had to look after the women and children and all we could do was pray for a miracle.

Father Kofi had become distant, depressed and even hostile after Father Kwesi's death. For weeks after burying him, Father Kofi would not mention Father Kwesi's name. It broke my heart to see him like that but any attempt I made to reach out was met with coldness and hostility, so I stopped and instead channeled my energies into helping the people where needed or when called upon. The day after I assisted in taking the Fanti people to the mission was the first time since the funeral that I had been on the mission, almost two months. I went to my office, opened the window, and stared over the river reflecting on all that had taken place to change our lives so drastically. I was soon aware of someone in the office and when I turned I saw Father Kofi.

We sat down and only then spoke about how much we missed Father Kwesi. I told him that I had sensed Father Kwesi near me one day as I smelled the perfume I had given him for Christmas. I told him I was not scared, and he replied, "I knew if he came back to visit anyone it would be you because the two of you were so close." Tears threatened but they remained unshed because I had never cried in front of anyone, and I was determined, even then, not to. Father Kofi then asked me to go to Father Kwesi's room and pack away his belongings. There was a safe in Father Kwesi's room where the money of various people in the parish as well as the parish funds were kept. Besides Father Kwesi I was the only other person who knew the combination to the safe. I told Father Kofi that I was honored to be given that privilege but I would go only if he accompanied me.

So together we went to Father Kwesi's room and packed up his clothes, books, and other personal belongings. These were to be taken to his family by Bishop Henry who planned to visit Ghana some time later that month. When that task was completed I opened the safe and took out everything. There were bundles of money belonging to various people. Father Kofi sat with me on the floor while I counted each bundle then handed it to him to decide how to dispense of it.

He needed to make some heart-wrenching decisions at that point. Those who had left their money in safe-keeping there had either run off or been killed. Father now had over fifty people to feed plus the few who trickled into the mission each day. I knew full well the question that was tormenting him. I looked at him deeply and saw his tortured soul mirrored in his eyes and I just held his hand and said consolingly, "God will understand, Father. You have to do what needs to be done."

Even if Father used some of the money to purchase whatever foodstuff was available to feed the Fanti people who sought refuge on the mission, it would not last very long. Some of them, especially the children, were very ill and needed medicine. They had only the clothes on their backs since everything else they owned had been taken away by the rebels. Their only hope was to be taken away from Greenville. Faith was all I had to live by during those days of trial and tribulation. I did not lose it and God did not disappoint me.

There was a community of Brothers residing in one of the towns close to Harper. Their mission was the envy of the town as it was well built, well equipped, and well cared for. These men of God were extremely generous and always shared their material goods with their fellow missionaries as well as the local people among whom they worked. After the rebel attack their communities in the U.S. and Europe collected foodstuff, clothes, and every possible item and sent a container for the three Brothers, Reuben, Donald, and Sean. Immediately they thought of us because they knew we were completely cut off from the rest of the country. Brother Donald was the most daring of the three and so he was the one who came bearing gifts.

Donald braved the harassment of the rebels on the five hour journey, and when we saw the blue truck with the large red cross painted on the door drive into the mission yard I knew that was the answer to my prayer and the hope of the Fanti people. We welcomed Donald with open arms and swiftly brought him up to date. Father Kofi pleaded with him to assist us to get the Fanti people out. Donald did not hesitate to agree.

After a brief rest and something to eat, the fifty odd members of the tribe on the mission were piled into the back of the truck and covered with the tarpaulin top. Brother Don had learned that the middle of the night was the best time for traveling. The rebels usually let the gates down and were either asleep or in a drunken stupor and didn't bother to stop or check on any vehicle. So as the dark slowly descended Brother drove off into the blackness of the night with the refugees safely hidden in the back.

We were anxious to get on the radio the next day and hear Brother Don's voice say he had arrived safely. We dared not mention his mission because the rebels now had some of the mission radios and we were sure they listened in on our conversations. But it was several months before I saw Brother and learned the fate of the Fanti people. On his way home Donald stopped at the home of a prominent member of the community in which the Brothers resided, a good and trusted friend of theirs, and explained his plight. She directed him to take a road through the forest that would bring him out to a certain point near the river separating Liberia from the Ivory Coast. She had canoes hidden nearby, and when she met Brother a short while later, she packed the Fanti women and children into the canoes and sent them over the river to safety on the other side.

Back in Greenville, Sister Angela, Doris, and I lived one day at a time, never knowing if the new day that dawned would be our last. We endured the sporadic outbursts of gunfire, which at times made us jump because it seemed to be coming from our backyard. The looting, burning, and arresting of civilians, who were either put in jail or executed, continued with alarming regularity.

We were surprised when Ben turned up to work one morning because we had no idea if he was dead or alive, and we were ever so grateful because none of the three of us was able to haul water from the well to fill the containers in the house. I had tried once and was almost pulled into the well when I swung the bucket down.

When Ben came to work at the convent he did not stray far from the building, because the rebels were using our yard as a thoroughfare. Each time we espied them, laden with their huge guns and with the most evil and cruel expressions on their faces, we would stand behind the door or window curtain so they couldn't see us. From our hiding places we watched until they had left the yard. It sickened me to feel so trapped and intimidated by these insurgents who had no idea of or respect for the law or justice but claimed that they were the new law of the land. We knew it was only a matter of time before they came and knocked on our front door, and we dreaded that time.

As the months flew by we had to live with the fact that the rebels were there to stay. They had now fully captured the entire southeast region of the country, as well as most of the northern region. These scruffy, untrained, uncontrollable rogues packing machine guns, AK7s or their favorite "Sister" Beretta ate marijuana like bread and drank "cane juice" (an unrefined, concentrated form of alcohol processed by men in the forest). They were cruel, irresponsible, and ignorant because some were merely children. Instead of preventing crimes and upholding the law they committed the most preposterous, unwarranted atrocities, which have never been recounted to the outside world.

All homes that were locked up when the owners ran into the forest were forcefully opened and entered by the rebels who either looted the belongings or occupied the house. The "officers" chose the nicest and best homes in the city area and installed themselves with their bodyguards and numerous concubines. It was amazing to see how the women and young girls surrounded and clung to these men as bees to honey. Many of the men and young boys had either freely joined the ranks while others were coerced into joining. So the only hope of these womenfolk abandoned by the menfolk was to co-habitate with the rebels.

There were many stories of young women being wounded or killed by the fighters whom they had befriended. One such incident occurred when the young woman was in bed with her rebel boyfriend. She began arguing with him about another young woman whom he was simultaneously seeing. The rebel flew into a rage, grabbed his loaded AK47 which was lying near the bed, aimed it at her face, and blew her head off. Another young woman was brought to the clinic with a huge hole in her arm. When questioned, she confessed that she was playing with her boyfriend's loaded weapon when it discharged straight into her arm.

Soon business at the clinic soared with the bulk of the patients being wounded fighters or civilians with gunshot or cutlass wounds inflicted by the rebels. One day Sister Angela returned to the convent with a sad and amazing story. That day a baby had been brought to the clinic with a hole right through his head. A policeman passing by a clump of palm trees had heard the loud wailing of a child. When he investigated he found the baby stuck through with one of the long, poisonous thorns that grew on those palm trees while its mother lay dead under the tree.

A man emerged from the bush and explained to the policeman that the rebels had killed the woman because she was of the wrong tribe, tore the baby from her arms, and flung it away. That's how it came to be stuck on the tree -- a most cruel and unbelievable story to the outside world but horribly true to those of us who had witnessed the cruelty and heartlessness of the rebels. While sister did her best to comfort the baby and ease the pain, infection had already stepped in and he soon died.

I who had always enjoyed a sound, undisturbed sleep rarely slept now but kept alert to the various sounds that filled the silence as darkness descended. I had become especially conscious of the sound of a bulldozer working relentlessly night after night, usually just after midnight until early dawn. It sounded as if it came from the beach area, always from the same direction. One day I questioned Ben who lived in Pool River, a village along the beach. Ben recounted a most horrendous tale that made me cover over my ears and shut my eyes as tightly as I could squeeze them. Every night civilians were being executed on the beach. The bulldozer was then used to dig shallow graves in the sand in which to dispose of the bodies. This was confirmed by people living along the beach who were traumatized by seeing the bodies being washed up in their front or backyards.

Greenville had been invaded by the rebels on July 26, 1990 and all the towns to the southern tip of Liberia followed thereafter. As the days turned into weeks and months, we watched helplessly as Greenville burst at the seams with people from all those different areas. While our own people had run into the forest and did not return, droves of men, women, and children from Monrovia, Zwedru, and other towns from the northern region flocked to Sinoe county.

They arrived by the truckloads, by canoes, by car, and some trekked for days and weeks until they arrived weak and starving on our doorsteps. Some had not even been aware that our town had been attacked. When their territory was attacked they ran with nothing save the clothes on their backs and traveled to wherever the wind took them. Meanwhile, swarms of fresh rebels kept arriving in new vehicles which they had stolen from the UN, UNICEF, the Red Cross, CRS, and other such agencies working in the country or cars and trucks hijacked from wealthy civilians.

The situation soon grew desperate. People, especially the old and very young, began to suffer from malnutrition. There was no food, especially rice, to feed the tens of thousands who had sought refuge in our county. Father Kofi was allowed to celebrate Mass once again and every Sunday our little church was packed to capacity. People of all faiths flocked to the Catholic church exhibiting their deep faith in God and trusting that he would take care of them. As starvation became imminent even for the sisters, Brother Donald once again came to our rescue. He teamed up with Sister Agnes, one of the sisters from a convent in Cape Palmas, and launched an appeal to a food agency in the United States to send supplies to the towns from Sinoe to Harper, the entire southern region, which included hundreds of thousands of people. Don and Agnes's plea was heard and soon they received the first shipment of rice and beans. There was just one small problem. The shipment arrived on the Ivory Coast so they had to find a way to get the supplies into Liberia and then to distribute them to the various towns and villages. First, they had to hire trucks to transport the rice from San Pedro to Tabu. Then they had to depend on the single rickety, most undependable ferry to get the trucks across and into Liberia. When they got into Liberia, the trucks took the supplies as far as the Brothers' compound in Pleebo -- if any managed to escape the thieving hands of the guards along the road in the Ivory Coast and those of the border patrols on either side of the river.

Many trials and tribulations faced Sister Agnes who personally cleared the cargo from the port in San Pedro then rode along with the trucks. There were several check points along the stretch of highway from San Pedro to Tabu, and each time Sister was besieged by intoxicated, senseless guards who drank gin like water. They gleefully looked forward to harassing the drivers and demanding the cargo. They attempted to humiliate Sister because she was female and because they thought she could not speak French. But, each time, when they made lewd remarks in French, she responded right back in French. She was not intimidated by the Ivorian military regime. She fought with an iron will to ensure that the food supplies for the starving people of Liberia reached its destination safely.

Once the supplies reached Pleebo, we had to find trucks to bring our share to Greenville. That's when Father Kofi and I tapped into the resources of the logging companies in our area. We soon came to depend on their trucks as the CRS "Rice Operation" grew to full capacity. Each time we brought a truckload from Pleebo, it was never enough to feed the multitudes. We had to find a way to do a census of the area and carry out fair distributions, but we had to find people who would not cheat. I soon solved that problem.

When I realized that Sunday service attendance had soared to great capacities I discussed with Father Kofi the possibility of beginning catechism classes both for children and adults. Before I had become a nun I was a member of the Legion of Mary, an organization of the Catholic Church dedicated to visiting the sick in the parish, seeking out old or fallen away members, and encouraging them to renew their commitment, as well as winning new members for the church. It was one of the few societies within the church in which I felt comfortable, and so in every parish that I worked, I had either been a member of the group if one existed, or began one.

St. Joseph's parish in Greenville was going to be no different. Although we did not have any of the usual paraphernalia to work with, I had deep faith that the Virgin Mary would understand and grace the meetings with her presence and blessings. When Father Kofi made the announcement that anyone wishing to receive instructions to become members of the Faith could come to these sessions, the response was overwhelming. The children met with Sister Doris and the adults came to me. I had close to fifty persons in my class, many of whom were students in the high school. We also invited members of the elders to meet with me to form a Legion of Mary club.

Hence, the faith of the people remained strong despite the rebels, the escalating rate of their atrocities, and the vicious nature of these crimes. In fact, the people's faith grew and this served to deepen mine. I began instructing and preparing my group of young adults to receive their First Communion as Catholics. This proved a bit sticky as I learned more about the lives of these young persons, some of whom were sixteen going on thirty. One of the rules in the Catholic Church states that persons who live together without being married could not receive Communion. Challenge number one -- I could not bend or break the rule but I didn't want to turn these faithful away. Sister Doris helped devise a palpable and comfortable situation.

Those who were living in relationships the church regarded as "sinful" were advised to separate. We assured everyone that we were not breaking up boyfriends and girlfriends but told what the Church required. Surprisingly, the few members of the class in common law relationships parted until they finished the classes and were able to make their First Communion.

Meanwhile, those who turned up for the Legion of Mary meetings numbered twelve. I called them the Twelve Apostles because they reminded me so much of the twelve men who followed Jesus. Those twelve men and women who met faithfully every Saturday afternoon in the church to recite the special prayers from the Legion handbook and the decades of the rosary were very simple, humble, ordinary men and women filled with a faith and zeal that I greatly admired. One of the important duties of a legionary was visiting the sick. The rule was that they be sent out in pairs -- and then an idea struck me. While they were doing their visitations, they could do a census of the city! I was warned that before anyone could venture out to do any kind of visitation I had to obtain the permission of the commanding officer of the rebels.

Commander Noreiga had taken up residence at the guest house on the port, and since Father Kofi was using our station wagon, I had to ask him to take me to visit the commander's camp. When I told Father Kofi of my plan he didn't want to take me but I insisted. When we drove into the yard that morning we were greeted by a great throng of people gathered there. As we disembarked from the car I sensed evil and death. The first sight that greeted our eyes was the white Corolla that had belonged to the Fathers, the very car in which Father Kwesi was killed by the rebels. It was riddled with bullet holes on both sides and in the back. I averted my eyes and turned to the side only to view a most appalling scene.

Lying on the dirt, clad only in a pair of briefs, was a man covered in dirt, spittle, blood, and other vile substances. The rebels were taking turns whipping, beating, jumping, and spitting on him. Each time he was hit he let out the most blood-curdling scream. Ironically, that man had been a rebel himself, but he had killed another man over a woman and that was the manner in which he was being publicly punished. No doubt he would eventually be killed, but at that point he didn't seem too far away from expiring by himself. I covered my ears and hid behind Father Kofi, but he moved aside so I could not avoid witnessing the horror while he exclaimed, "Well, you wanted to come, didn't you? So don't be shy to face the music now!" I hated him for being so cruel but I remained silent.

As we came to the front door of the house we were greeted by Noreiga himself. I had never seen or met him before, and as I beheld the man who had caused such fear and hatred, I could not help but admire his grand appearance. He was very tall, well built, and rather handsome. He had a very captivating smile and exuded charm. But I was not fooled, because I had heard that even while he was smiling sweetly he could order that someone in his presence be shot. Father Kofi greeted him humbly and seemed to grow even more docile while Noreiga looked me over from my head down to my toes.

I remained outwardly calm, serious and firm, as I looked him full in the eyes. He shook my confidence momentarily when he told me that I was from the Caribbean. I dared to ask him how he knew, and he smiled charmingly but coldly and replied, "Ah, Sister, you'd be surprised how much I know. I studied this city and all its inhabitants, which includes you and the other two nuns, before I ventured here, and there's nothing I don't know about any of you!" I suspected he was bluffing but I felt the hair stand on my arms and neck.

I looked meaningfully at Father Kofi, hoping he would recognize my signal to obtain what we had come for and then get the hell out of that place. Noreiga, however, would not give us the chance to speak. He gushed on about his having trained in the Cuban army under Fidel Castro and of his having fought in the Gulf war. Then he spoke with relish about his many raids and conquests of various villages in the county. He claimed that he had killed thousands and had always returned with proof (arms, fingers, ears, and even the heads of people who had perished under his hands).

I complimented him on his achievement and then quickly asked the permission for my legionaries to go visiting. He looked at me intently and his only comment, which I recognized as a veiled threat, was, "Now, just make sure that they wear proper identification and do only church work. I hope I wouldn't have to make an example of any of them, including you!" My blood chilled at the eerie sound of his remark and the underlying message and I wished then that I had wings to take immediate flight. Instead I steeled myself and endured his "smart talk" with Father Kofi. After a few moments, Father glanced my way and saw my discomfort, so he hastily bid Noreiga farewell.

As soon as I returned to the convent I gathered markers and paper and set about making name tags for each member of the team who would be going out to visit the homes in the town. We had a meeting scheduled for two that afternoon, and when I got to the church I stamped each name tag with the official stamp of the parish. When the members arrived a few minutes later, I distributed the tags and recounted my bizarre meeting with the commander. I sternly warned each member to be careful when they made their visits and gathered information for a census of the city.

I accompanied a different team each day as they visited their assigned area and trained them to ask the appropriate questions while I took notes. By the end of the first month I had visited every nook and cranny of the town of Greenville. I had walked on every street, trudged through dust, dirt, mud, bushes taller than I was, and crossed a river in a canoe to visit every home in the area. Father Kofi did not accompany us nor did he offer to take us in the car even though he had the Sisters' car. I was pretty angry about that, but I said nothing. In fact I refused to speak to Father for a few weeks until I was able to work through my anger, but the close friendship we had previously shared was no more.

I resented Father's behavior, which had become extremely wanton and quite immoral. I did not think that it was my duty or place to condemn him, but he was being openly offensive. On many days when I would be weak and tired from walking, I would espy Father whizzing past me in our car filled with women or with his friends as he drove about having a good time. Women, both young and old, frequented the mission and were even found sleeping there, and what angered me the most was when I discovered that Father was giving the rice to all his girl-friends. We stored the supplies on the mission and he was the only one with the key. I never suspected until one day I unexpectedly dropped in on the mission and caught him in the act.

I ignored Father and his dreadful actions and instead channeled my energies into helping the people as I went about visiting homes. I was able to obtain first-hand information of the situation and see exactly what the rebels had done. I was appalled, horrified, and saddened how those self-acclaimed "commandos" harmed, humiliated, and stripped innocent, unprotected, and unarmed civilians. Some civilians had remained throughout the attack because they had nowhere to go. When their farms were stripped and their household livestock stolen they were forced to travel into the villages to seek foodstuff like rice, cassava, pepper, dried meat, and any other commodities they could find.

Their nightmare was relived each time they came to one of the several checkpoints. The rebels interrogated, searched, and then filched the produce these people had trekked miles and miles to obtain. Not satisfied they then set about to strip the men and take away their clothes and shoes, beat them up, and even assault the women. Civilians were completely at the mercy of these ruffians who proclaimed themselves the law of the land. There was no one to protect them, and anyone who tried was threatened by Noreiga and his "warriors."

One day a truck packed with civilians leaving Greenville was stopped at a checkpoint guarded by extremely cruel rebels. The soldiers randomly chose men whom they made an example of. That particular day one man was singled out and dragged off the truck. He was pushed to the ground, punched and kicked at the orders of Noreiga himself, who was at the gate. He then set upon Peter, the civilian being beaten, forced open his mouth with the butt of a gun which was then inserted into his mouth and pounded, thus smashing Peter's teeth and the interior of his mouth. The women began to scream, and one boy jumped down and ran quickly to the mission to summon Father Kofi because

Peter was a prominent member of the church.

When Father Kofi arrived on the scene, he pleaded with Noreiga to spare Peter's life. Peter's face was covered in blood and so badly smashed it was unrecognizable. After freeing Peter, Noreiga regarded Father Kofi coldly and banefully declared, "You always begging for others, when is your turn I will see who will beg for you!" Father realized then that he was just as vulnerable and unsafe as every other civilian to the attacks of that madman.

Noreiga frequently visited the mission to use Father's ham radio and Father was helpless to stop him. They had long conversations about everything and everybody, including the sisters. Father told me that Noreiga was very interested in us and what we did, particularly me. Father warned me to be careful because Noreiga "has his eye on you," but I assured him that I was not susceptible to the man's charms.

As the days progressed and I ventured out farther and farther to do my visitation rounds I encountered the rebels everywhere. They were always very polite and civil to me and those in vehicles would offer me a ride, but I always gently refused no matter how weary I was. I had to be extremely diplomatic in my dealings with them. I didn't want to seem over-friendly, but God forbid if I was rude or offended them, thus incurring their wrath, particularly that of their commander. Many of my students had joined forces with the rebels, and what affected me the most was the sight of boys ten and twelve years old or even younger walking around trying to look fierce and carrying guns almost as big as they were.

One day Sister Doris came to my room in a state of panic. She had seen three boys carrying guns walking up the path to the convent. Sister was really scared but I assured her that no harm would come to us. We stood by the window and watched them approach the house, but instead of going to the front door they went around to the back. Our back door off the laundry room led out into the garage. Sister and I hurried silently through the corridor and stood behind the door awaiting their next move. We both jumped nervously when we heard the soft rap. Sister stood behind me as I removed the bar then undid the three bolts. I was shaking but if it was our turn to die, well, so be it. My heart went out with pity and compassion for the three baby-faced boys before me. They looked weary, hungry, sick, and so, so sad. I assured Sister Doris that it was all right so she came forward and the boys immediately greeted us ever so politely then said, "Sister, we hungry, can we please have a piece of bread to eat?" Sister and I looked at each other, astonished at their politeness and almost gentlemanly behavior. We asked them to wait while we brought out three folding chairs which we placed in the garage. We watched them unhook their guns from around their shoulders and place them on the ground before they sat down.

Sister had boiled a pot of rice earlier and without hesitation emptied half of it into a large bowl and added red palm oil, salt, pepper, and dried fish, making a mixture which we knew all Liberians enjoyed. Sister had now lost all fear of the boys. She placed three spoons in the bowl and took it out to them while I mixed a jug of powdered milk and followed her out with three glasses and the jug. When we placed the food and drink in front of them, we were again surprised to see them bow their heads and say grace before partaking of it. As they hungrily devoured the contents of the bowl we chatted with them.

They each told us their name and explained that they were not from our county but were captured in Nimba county and forced to join forces with the rebels. One of them, Robert, was ten years old and had a gruesome tale to tell. He said that his mother, who was pregnant and her six children were captured when the rebels attacked their area. The rebels decided to have some fun and began to wager whether the baby was a male or female. The leader of the band of murderers insisted that he was correct. To prove his point he pulled out a knife and split the woman's abdomen, then snatched the baby out as her shocked children looked on in horror. The dead woman and her unborn child were simply thrown out the back door while the rebels ransacked the house. The children scattered and began to seek out places to hide. Robert, however was captured and made to join the rebels under the threat of a death like his mother's. Sister Doris wept silently but I was overcome with anger. Robert remained quite stoic and bravely declared that he had joined because he intended to seek out those who had killed his mother and her baby and kill them.

The other two boys revealed that they had been students in the Catholic school in Nimba, which explained their excellent manners and good training. Sister Doris counseled the boys, giving them some sound, godly advise, and then we told them that it was time they said good-bye. They were reluctant to leave, but we told them that it was time for us to go inside and say our prayers. As we went inside and closed the door behind us, we looked out the window and watched as they made their way down the same path they had trod about two hours earlier. After that day the rebels came to the convent at any time of day or night.

One night around eleven o'clock I heard an urgent knock on my door. When I opened the door Sister Angela stood before me and infuriatingly declared, "Some of your people are at the front door. You'd better go and see what they want and could you please tell them not to come to the convent at this hour!" I was angered at the tone of her voice and her insinuation that the rebels, whom she referred to as "your people" had come to visit me. I picked my way in the dark until I reached the window next to the front door. In the shadows I could identify the outline of a few of the rebels.

Assuming my most severe voice, I scolded the rebels for disturbing and scaring the nuns. I informed them that they could not come to the convent whenever they pleased but should wait until daylight to seek whatever they wanted. "Please, Sister, we are really sorry to disturb you, but you have nothing to fear from us. It's just that my men are extremely ill with the fever and headache, can we please have some aspirins?" their leader gently pleaded. I was continually encountering the rebels as I did my rounds of visitations and had spoken to a few of the men, who had revealed their typical day. Between the interminable pounding of guns being fired, going hungry for days, trudging through pouring rain and sweltering sun, through forest, lagoons, ravines, swamps, and rivers as they conquered new grounds, it was no wonder that these men were as sick as dogs.

The group of rebels in the jeep outside our front door was a new group that had recently entered Greenville and their leader was Malcolm. I had seen him driving around and had been greeted politely and offered a ride. After inquiry, I had learned that he had been a prominent member of the Nimba county and most who encountered him could not understand how such a kind, soft-spoken, well-mannered gentleman could have become involved in the cause of the National Patriotic Front of Liberia.

In all conscience I could not let his plea go unheeded. Sister Angela kept a cupboard of medicine in the convent for emergencies, and this was certainly an emergency. I ran quickly to the cupboard and took out two cans of aspirins, a can of antibiotics, and some stomach medicine. I brought these to the front door, unlocked it, and handed them to Malcolm. He thanked me profusely and offered to pay for them but I suggested that he take the men to the clinic the next day so they could be examined by Sister Angela. Then they could pay her there. All the men joined Malcolm in saying good-bye, and when they left I quickly closed the heavy oak door, bolted it and collapsed against it, trembling with fright.

The twelve members of the Legion of Mary had covered the whole of Greenville City visiting, bringing the word of God and comfort to all whom they met, and also gathered information for a census of the city. By the time we found trucks to bring the first supply of rice and beans to Greenville, I had made and distributed ration cards for households to collect the food. In the beginning it was supposed to be only for the old and the very young but we were continually confronted with a growing population of displaced hungry and near starving men, women, and children of all ages.

The food that arrived was never enough. Bringing the bags of rice, beans, and corn meal from Pleebo to Sinoe was an extremely perilous task that varied from carefully maneuvering the treacherous roads to appeasing the irrational, demanding, countless "commandos" encountered along the way. After many an ambush by rebels, flat tires, and near tragic accidents, the trucks were able to arrive in Greenville with the meager supplies. Distribution was done only on certain days, but once the food arrived and was stored in the school, the campus was packed every day with people requesting supplies. It was heartbreaking for me to turn away those who did not have ration cards because the supplies were not meant for them. I felt the anger, frustration, and hunger of these people but I could not alleviate any of their pain.

In the middle of our struggle we got word that Sister Agnes was being recalled by her community in the United States and Father Kofi's bishop requested his return to Ghana. That was December 1990, and there was no sign of an end of the civil war. In fact, things grew worse as the atrocities increased. Ironically, the members of the peacekeeping force sent to maintain some semblance of civility were also guilty of atrocities like looting, raping women, killing innocent civilians, and all the other horrific acts committed by the rebels.

These were things I was accustomed to reading about that happened in other countries. It was impossible to believe that I was now deep in the midst of it and witnessing the horrors of death in every form each day. Those who did not die by the gun or the knife died from starvation or illness.

Father Kofi left Sinoe on his birthday, the last day of the year, so we began the New Year without a priest. The bishop announced that we would be getting a new pastor, but we did not know when he would arrive because he was in the United States on a Mission Appeal.

Sister Doris and I continued holding Communion services in the church and endeavored to reopen the school. We advertised the beginning of a Bible School and invited all the children and youths to attend. As they came forward to register, no one could afford to pay the fee previously charged so we decided on a minimal amount that everyone could afford. Sister and I decided that whatever money we collected would be used to pay the handful of teachers. Against growing odds we resumed classes in January. We knew very well that we had to be extremely careful about what we imparted during classes. Sister and I warned the teachers and vigilantly screened every lesson plan before it reached the classroom. Despite our timid beginning we proceeded with careful confidence-not flaunting ourselves in anyone's face- and gained strength as we progressed. Several times groups of rebels visited the campus, but I always confronted them before they got any farther than the front door of the office. I suspected that they had come to spy and see exactly what was taking place and I acted like I had nothing to hide.

In late February, Bishop Henry got word to us that the new priest, Father Joseph, would be arriving in April. I had never met him but had heard that he was vocal and unafraid of conflict. April began but no Father Joe. Easter came and went but still no Father Joe. I did a small distribution of rice just before Easter and was almost killed because I could not satisfy the multitudes that flocked the campus. Brother Don drove the blue truck that brought the limited sacks of rice and beans, and on his return to Pleebo I decided to go with him. I was exhausted, extremely undernourished, and badly in need of a vacation.

I spent the night in Pleebo, then bright and early the next day Brother took me to the border to ride the ferry over to the Ivory Coast where I would stay for a time. As I crossed over and reached the Ivorian border I was greeted by one of the sisters who was accompanied by Father Joe. He had just returned from the United States and would soon be on his way to Greenville. I don't quite remember how I looked at him or greeted him, but he told me when I returned to Greenville about a month later that I did not give him the time of day. I believed him because the moment I got out of Liberia I did not want to think of the place again and dreaded the day I would have to return.

I spent the first two weeks recuperating at a convent in Tabu. The sisters there were all elderly and spoke only French. There was one who spoke English but she spent her time at the outstation she was in charge of in one of the villages. I was pale, thin, and exhausted. I spent the first week locked in my bedroom where I cried until I fell into a deep sleep. The sisters were concerned, but in between periods of sleep, I assured them that I was all right. They kept attempting to fill me up with food, but I discovered that my stomach had shrunk and refused to take real solid food. I gave in to the depression that had plagued me for months instead of fighting it for another minute. I knew that was the only way I was going to be rid of it and be healed.

Spiritually, I felt completely estranged from God. I went through the motions of the traditional prayers I was required to say daily, but it was a long time since I had truly prayed. I used the example of St. Therese as my meditation and found great comfort in it. She was a young woman who became a nun against profound opposition. She was just fifteen, but was convinced that she wanted to become a nun. In the convent she was treated badly by the superior and then began experiencing extreme spiritual "dryness." She wrote that Jesus was playing "hide and seek" with her and had not really abandoned her. She expressed great confidence that he would eventually reveal himself and his great love for her, so she patiently endured whatever pain, suffering, and frustration he sent her.

I felt devoid of all emotions because I had hardened my heart and steeled myself from feeling anything for anyone during those months and the traumatic experiences I had been exposed to. There was no telephone at the convent in Tabu, and I badly wanted to communicate with my family. After a week I felt strong enough to venture out. I told the Superior that I wanted to take a bus into San Pedro, a nearby town that was more developed than Tabu, so that I could telephone my parents. She told me that she would be driving there in a day or two so I could go with her. I did that, and as soon as we got to the convent in San Pedro, I greeted the sisters there and went straight to the telephone.

Hearing my mother describe her anxiety and fears for me as well as for the other two sisters tugged at my heart and made me realize how much I missed my precious family. I had missed seeing my nieces grow up. I had acquired a new niece whom I did not even know. I did not see the sense in our having to stay in the midst of a civil war that had nothing to do with us, but such were the orders of the Superior, and I had taken a vow of obedience so stay I did. My parents were receiving explicit details of the war as seen in Monrovia and reported on CNN, but there were no reports about the other parts of Liberia. It was as if the war was only in Monrovia, which was ravaged by the scourge that had been inflicted upon the whole country. How wrong that report was!

After three weeks on the Ivory Coast, I received word that Sister Jane, our Superior, was arriving with Sister Monica, the fourth Sister for our mission in Liberia. Sister Monica was from the same country as I was, but had served on the missions for most of her religious life. She was the principal of a school run by the sisters in one of the islands, but was contracted by the government, so had to remain until her contract was up. Not that she minded, because she was reluctant to accept her assignment to Liberia and had to be coerced until she finally agreed after one year and some months. Sister was a very happy and friendly person. She was a seasoned missionary with an open and easy manner. Everyone felt that she would fit right in with the people of Greenville. Yet she was skeptical about her assignment to Liberia.

When we crossed over into Liberia Sister was appalled by the many guns. Her fear grew as we journeyed to Greenville. I had to sit at the back of the truck since there was no room at the front. I was wrapped from head to toe in a lappa to protect my skin from the red dirt. Each time we arrived at one of the checkpoints, the soldiers swarmed around the truck, but before they could molest the sisters or take the luggage at the back, I stood up, unwrapped my face, and greeted them. Most of the rebels were familiar with me by then and knew I did not fear them or the weapons they bore, so they fell back.

We arrived in Greenville in time to reopen the school which had been closed for the Easter season. Only then did it occur to me that I had been loath to return and I again had to shake the sadness and depression that was threatening to settle on me. Sister Monica assumed her place as principal of the junior high school. She cleared out the principal's desk, used by a man who had run off and abandoned his post. We had not heard further from him so had no idea if he was dead or alive. Sister Monica was warmly welcomed and readily accepted and loved by all the students.

Father Joseph had been installed as the new parish priest of Greenville. The first thing he did was to approach Malcolm, the new general of the rebels, requesting the return of the car that belonged to the mission. When Father Kofi left, he returned the wagon to the sisters but we were advised to park it in the garage and remove the tires and other parts because the rebels would be sure to walk in and demand that we give it to them. Father was given a runaround but eventually retrieved the white Corolla in which Father Kwesi had been killed. Since the key had been thrown away, the rebels had improvised so that it was not necessary to use a key to start it.

For the first few months I refused to sit in it. And for many days I was sick and weak from malaria fever, but I would steel myself and walk from the school to the convent. One day, however, I almost passed out in school and had to allow Father

Joseph to take me in the car. Father Joseph was a warm, easy-going, humble, hardworking man. I immediately felt drawn to him, and we became fast friends. I invited him to teach religion in the Bible School and he readily accepted. He was more open to new ideas than the other priests had been and so the sisters worked more easily with him.

After a few months he was joined by Brother Roland, a Liberian who was a member of a religious community from Monrovia. All the other members were foreigners and were soon recalled to their various homelands, but Brother Roland had been abandoned and had nowhere to seek refuge. Because Greenville was vast and the work heavy, Father Joe readily accepted the bishop's suggestion that Brother Roland assist. Thus he arrived in Greenville and was soon loved by all. He had been part of a teaching community in Monrovia so I immediately requested his assistance in the school, much to his delight.

Around that time a group of health officials working in Monrovia began traveling through the other regions of Liberia meeting with all missionaries working in schools or involved in education in any form. They first counseled us, then trained us to counsel the youths to deal with life after the war and their many traumatic experiences. Various programs were discussed to detraumatize them. One was using the school as an outlet but not further stressing them out with heavy academic studies. We were advised to make the atmosphere more light and relaxing. Once they were willing to return to school we had to invent interesting and innovative ways to keep them there and encourage them to learn and want to stay.

To maintain such an atmosphere a curriculum was built around teaching basic subjects like mathematics, English, religion and social studies with the rest of the time interspersed with French, singing, typing and indoor and outdoor sports. Father Joe taught religion, Brother Roland took charge of the sports, I hired two male teachers who taught math and social studies and I was responsible for the other subjects. Father, Brother, and I as much as possible counseled the students when they came to us or when the opportunity presented itself.

In my English class I varied sessions as much as possible. I taught them to play Scrabble to teach spelling, and devised a game where one person would come up with a particular letter of the alphabet and the rest of the class had to guess the names of a list of chosen items beginning with that letter. The first student to finish the list shouted "Stop!" and everyone had to put down pens or pencils. Points were given to real words, spelling, etc. Father encouraged lively debates in his religion classes as he discussed subjects interesting and relevant to the lives of the young people, all the while imparting sound doctrine and deep lessons of faith. Brother, being more active, organized them into teams to play volleyball, basketball, kickball, and other sports at which the students excelled.

Since neither Father Joe nor Brother Roland needed an office in the school, I was able to transform the first room into a small library. The senior class assisted in this transformation. They obtained planks of wood that had been lying around the mission, painted them, as well as concrete blocks, and used them to build shelves. Next we brought over the books from the book room in the junior school and arranged them on the shelves according to subject matter. Then I cataloged every single book and magazine and stamped it with the school stamp. There was a very large table outside the room and I set this up as a reading table. One student was assigned to hand out books and ensure their return. To encourage students to read, I assigned book reports and special assignments. It filled my heart with such pride in my students to see them huddling around that table after school, pouring over books.

Typing classes began in the afternoon only after they had completed their chores. I divided up the entire campus into various areas and each grade - ten, eleven and twelve - was responsible for cleaning a particular area. As an incentive I gave out prizes for the best kept and cleanest areas and had no problem in getting them to do their share of cleaning. The prizes were commodities that I knew the students badly needed and could not obtain because there were no shops open at that time. They therefore turned to the sisters for everything, but I did not want to simply hand things out. My philosophy was "Work never killed and maintained the dignity of the human," so I made them "work" for what they needed.

Simon, the mission boy, had taught me to make the blue soap that the Liberians loved for washing their clothes. After the war, when no other type was available, the people began using that soap for bathing. When they could not obtain it, they went without washing themselves and their clothes. So I learned to make the soap and used it sparingly as prizes, or after they had completed some task satisfactorily. In teacher training, my lecturer had emphasized the method of rewarding good behavior. After applying that psychology for a few weeks, negative behavior became almost a thing of the past.

By no means did I suddenly find myself with a band of angels, but my students knew me and my way. One day I overheard one student remarking to another: "Me, I don't want to cross Sister-O, when she vex with you the way she can look at you and ignore you can really hurt your heart, yah!" I laughed to myself and thought how well they knew me. I had never hit a student in all my years of teaching and was not about to, but I had to devise ways to punish their wrongdoing.

What I detested most was an insolent or disobedient student, and there were a few of those. Whenever they were rude to me, or anyone, for that matter, I would give them a solid tongue-lashing and then totally ignore them, excluding them from class sessions and other activities. Within minutes of that kind of treatment, most were filled with remorse and apologized, swearing that they would never be rude or disrespectful again. I would often warn the students that even though they were men and women in their home environments, when they entered the campus of St. Joseph's, they were mere students and had to be obedient. If they chose to bring their surliness into the classroom, then I had no choice but to send them home -- and I did in fact suspend and even expel a few. I wanted the best for them and gave my all, but I was not prepared to put up with any nonsense from any of them.

I had begun another class preparing students for First Communion, many of which were students at the high school. When the day drew near for them to be received into that aspect of the Church, I asked Father Joe to give them a retreat. He suggested having a healing service for all the students since they could certainly benefit from it. I readily agreed, and so together with Brother Roland planned a special day for all the students. The high school had almost eighty students, and each one-Catholic or otherwise-was invited to participate. We began early in the morning gathering in the largest of the three classrooms. Brother and I took turns leading them in song and prayer until it was Father's turn to give his talk.

Father Joseph was puny in stature, but when he opened his mouth, everyone stopped whatever they were doing and listened attentively. And that morning was no exception. Father spoke as if possessed by the Holy Spirit. Both Brother and I sat awestruck and took in every word that fell from Father's mouth. I stole a glance around the room and observed the students. Some were openly weeping and others I could see were deeply touched. He edified the students, comforted them, and then challenged them with his message. After preaching for almost two hours, everyone was invited to go to Confession.

Confession is one of the seven sacraments of the Catholic Church and is not practiced by other religions. Father explained that those who were not Catholic did not have to partake if they did not wish, but if they felt the need to discuss any aspect of their lives, they were welcome to visit him. He then made his way to the classroom next door which had been prepared for that purpose, and while students made themselves ready by examining their conscience, as is the custom before Confession, we sang appropriate hymns very softly and meaningfully and prayed the rosary. I knelt on the cold concrete floor and prayed continuously as student followed student visiting Father for Confession. I was so moved I had to fight back the tears. It was well into the evening before every student had been to see Father, then Brother and I took our turns. I could not believe the impact that service had on the students. Girls and boys wept openly and a certain softness appeared on their faces, even on the face of the class rogues and the most arrogant and troublesome students.

That evening, as the sisters met for supper, I was eager to share the experience with them but we faced a dilemma. During the months that Sister Monica had been there she had seemed to be happy, but at the same time had grown rather silent and reserved. I knew that was unlike her, but I assumed she was having a little trouble adjusting and settling in. A few days before she had succumbed to a bout of malaria, but instead of overcoming it as Sister Doris and I did when we got the attacks, she fell more and more ill. It was as if overnight she had aged. She had grown exceptionally emaciated, having come to Liberia a plump, jolly figure. I went to visit her in her room that evening and she kept pleading, "Please get me out of here, please don't let me die in this place!"

I resolved that night to speak to Father Joseph the next day and have him come and pray with her. I had also hoped that he could hold more healing services, perhaps one every month and wanted to discuss that possibility with him as well. However, when I arrived at the mission the next day, the place was alive with excitement. Father immediately summoned me to his house when I arrived in my office and broke the news to me. A shipment of food supplies was arriving at the port of Greenville within the next few days and we were asked to be responsible for storing and distributing it. Father suggested using the classrooms of the high school to store the foodstuff and enlisting the students to assist with the distribution.

167

Father and Brother both confessed that they had no experience with that operation, but I had, so they asked if I would organize the necessary teams. Oh yes, I had tons of experience in organizing and managing such an operation and was pretty efficient at it, but I detested the person I became under such undue stress and tension. And if we were expecting a shipment, then the operation was going to be a lot larger than the ones I had previously done. Nevertheless, being the good, obedient, efficient nun that I was, I rolled up my sleeves and plunged headlong into the necessary preparations prior to the much anticipated and needed arrival of the vessel.

Without any doubt the students were thrilled that classes would have to be suspended indefinitely and went out their way to assist. The first thing we did was remove all the desks from the rooms. They were taken over to the junior school and stored in the auditorium. Then planks of wood were placed on the floor to protect the sacks that would be laid there. As reports came in about areas that had not been visited and the people counted, teams were assigned to do the necessary work, and when they returned with the information obtained, ration cards were prepared and distributed.

Able-bodied men were needed to transport the sacks from the trucks and stack them in the classrooms. I immediately sent out a notice inviting honest, robust, strong men to work. There was no money to pay them but they would be rewarded with a certain amount of rice. Hundreds of men, young and old, feeble and strong, honest and thieving, turned up on the campus the next day. Each was carefully screened and given a task. Those who could not carry a sack of rice on their backs were told to guard the doors, keep the lines in order or do other less strenuous tasks necessary for the smooth running of the operation. Only the male students would be allowed in the distribution room with Brother, Father, and me to fill the sacks which the people would provide to collect their rations.

Soon I was caught up in the fever pitch that pervaded the

whole city, and at last the day came when I stood on the port to receive the ship with its precious cargo. I was invited on board to meet the captain and I seized that opportunity to request a necessary and important favor. I was convinced that there was a telephone aboard. There was one, and I could make a call. My time was long overdue for a vacation. Sister Jane had purchased a ticket for me to journey to England that summer and stay for as long as I wanted. I was determined to find a way out of Liberia for Sister Monica whose condition was fast deteriorating. She had stopped eating, could barely walk, and was weak and depressed all the time. I was really afraid that she was going to die. So I had made up my mind to let her use my ticket, but of course, I could not make that decision by myself; I needed to obtain the permission of the Superior.

As soon as I had cleared the cargo on board, Father got the designated team into motion and I slipped away quickly to the engine room where I was allowed to call Sister Jane. I awakened her from a deep sleep but I spoke sternly to rouse her so she would listen carefully and understand what I was saying. I told her how sick Sister Monica was and then told, not asked her, that I was giving Sister my ticket to travel to England to get immediate medical attention. Sister listened attentively, agreed wholeheartedly, and thanked me for allowing Sister to travel in my place. The next step was to get Sister over to the Ivory Coast to board the plane. That was easily taken care of the very next day.

The agency that was responsible for sending the rice to us also provided volunteer workers and vehicles. Some of them had to travel to the Ivory Coast to do business, so two days later, Sister Monica packed up all that she had brought with her and left Liberia to travel to England to receive medical treatment for whatever was ailing her. We were sad to say good-bye to her, but it was a blessing that she got out when she did. We lived with the hope that she would return one day when she was healed, but of course, she never did.

The "rice operation" was plagued with problems from start to finish. I was constantly confronting men who had stolen the rice and hidden it in various places, and the trucks were stopped and the men guarding the rice beaten up or arrested because they would not give the rice to the soldiers. Then families were constantly increasing the number on their ration cards by claiming absent relatives who did not really exist or adding neighbors' children to their own. I visited all the homes that seemed to have more people than when we originally visited them and I tore up cards when I found that they were cheating. Some people were so brazen even when their dishonesty was discovered that they cursed and threatened me, but I stood my ground and showed them that I did not scare easily.

Some of them asked me if the rice was mine and I replied that it wasn't but I was appointed guardian and because I believed in fairness and justice, I was going to see that everyone was served fairly even if I were killed in the process. I had my veil torn from my head, I was cuffed in the face, my car was stoned, and received threats from people whom I had disgraced by exposing their dishonesty and greed, but I did not lose heart or give up. When those people saw my determination grow instead of weaken, they began referring to me as "that bad 'oman!" Father Joseph and Brother Roland were for their part plagued relentlessly by persons requesting "favors." Their integrity was put to the test and they were challenged in every possible way by those in the community, even prominent church members, to favor them above their own brothers and sisters.

Despite these problems, the first distribution on such a large scale took place over a period of one week. We zoned off the city and served a particular area each day. While the male students assisted in filling the sacks, buckets, pillow sacks, bowls, and whatever else the people brought to collect their ten, twenty or thirty cups of rice, beans, corn meal, and even cans of meat, the female students lit a fire at the back of the school and prepared large pots of rice, greens, beans, and the likes to feed every person who worked during that operation on the campus.

I did lose my temper many times. When the people refused to line up in an orderly fashion, I stood on the window with a broom in my hand and threatened to stick anyone who pushed the people around them, made noises or behaved like an animal. I received no more complaints or problems after that. When the students grew lazy and refused to work fast enough with the distribution, I myself lifted a sack of rice that weighed one hundred and 110 pounds and threw it out the window and sometimes I stormed off in frustration seeking refuge in my office where I let off steam by dissolving into tears. But regardless of all this, I had fun with my students. We laughed, prayed, sang, teased, criticized in a friendly way as we grew into a closely-knit family. When the distributions were over for that week, I organized a picnic on the beach for all the students. There we were able to relax and take a breather until the next distribution came around.

During the weeks that followed, each day a new group of people turned up on the mission claiming that we had missed their area. We then realized that we would have to venture into the remote villages beyond the city where people had escaped and were living in very squalid conditions. Father saw the need to broaden the teams. He had recently been chosen to head an ecumenical council in the county and felt that he could embrace that opportunity to set an example of the "brotherhood" he preached. He thus chose the ministers and members of the other churches to join the various teams that were already established. I did not support this decision and proved my point when various problems emerged.

Many of those "men of the cloth" whom Father had chosen and given responsibility for certain areas were men who could not be trusted. They used their positions to control the people whom they bribed, cheated, sold ration cards to, and gave extra cards in return for sexual and other favors. They revealed the greed, selfishness, dishonesty, and fraudulent behavior I had expected of my students. Whenever a report was brought to

Father Joseph, he simply ignored it, and this angered and frustrated me, but I soon found a way to overcome it. I warned my students to be on guard for occasions of cheating or fraud and they became my sleuths. Whenever they obtained proof, we would all confront Father, and after a while he could no longer turn a deaf ear and blind eye to those who were responsible for the negative behavior. Tactfully, he relieved them of the positions which they were using for evil instead of good. Threats of all kinds were hurled at the students but no one dared say anything to me or wish any of their "ju ju" on me.

One day while I was in my office Simon came and knocked on the door which was ajar. I called him in and invited him to sit, but he said he would remain standing. He looked extremely nervous and embarrassed and kept his eyes downcast. I asked, "What's wrong Simon, you know you can tell me anything." He finally asked my permission to visit the clinic. I asked him if it was a serious matter, and he barely whispered, "Yes, Sis." I didn't press further since I sensed his discomfort, so I quickly penned a note to Sister Angela to attend to his medical needs and sent him off.

He returned a few hours after and came straight to the office. This time he sat down. He reported that Sister had given him an injection "that stung like pepper" and some antibiotics to drink. He was supposed to return to brush grass around the clinic because he had no money to pay for the treatment. I then gently but firmly coaxed: "Simon, look at me, what did Sister say?" Simon wrapped his arms around his stomach, shook his head violently from side to side, and bawled like a baby. "Oh God, Sis, she say I have gonorrhea and I going to die!" I knew Sister must have been disappointed and angry that Simon had gotten himself in such a mess and said that to scare him. Yet I felt the blood drain from my body. I just sat very still and let him cry while I attempted to compose myself.

I remembered something my mother had said to me when I was a teenager and I realized then how true her remark was. I didn't have a lot of friends and didn't go to parties a lot, but every time I did go I made sure my mother knew who was taking me and bringing me back home. Yet whenever I returned, she would always be waiting up. One night after returning from a friend's wedding I said, "Mummy, you know you can trust me and you know Sandra and her family, so why did you wait up?" My mother looked at me and wisely replied, "One day when you are a mother or in a position of a mother, you'll understand!" Now, sitting in that office confronted with the seriousness of the situation involving someone whom I considered my own child, I knew exactly what my mother meant.

My heart felt as if it were being ripped out. My whole body burned feverishly and I felt so weak I dared not attempt to stand. I had never had any experience in sexual matters but I read up on the subject so I could educate my students. I warned them, both male and female, about the consequences of giving in to passion. I often had open discussions in my religion and catechism classes, but soon realized that they knew more about sex than I did. I therefore attacked the topic from another angle. If they were already practicing sex I could not tell them to stop. I did try, and one student was bold enough to remark, "Sister, we not nuns and priests you know!" So all I could do and did do was warn them to be careful.

In between his body-wracking sobs Simon blurted out: "Oh God, Sis, I should have listened to you, I should have been more careful, sorry, Sister!" I didn't bother to question why he was sorry but I guessed it was because he was feeling guilty. I did not admonish because I knew he was in enough pain. I wanted to find out who the girl was so she could be treated as well. I knelt by the chair and held his hand, and after a long while his sobs subsided. Then I ventured to ask, "Simon, please tell me who the girl is, she needs to receive treatment quickly so no one else gets infected." I was rendered speechless when he agonizingly replied, "Sister, I don't even know her name."

I was angry that he could be so careless and foolish but at the same time I was relieved that it was not one of our female students. He went on to explain that he had met the girl who was from another village when their football team came to play our team in Greenville. As he spoke, I suddenly remembered seeing him that Sunday afternoon with some strange girl. The football field was a few miles behind the convent, and the students knew how much I enjoyed a good game so whenever there was a match they would come to the convent and invite me to walk over to the field with them. I reminded him of that incident and asked him if it was the same girl, and he said yes. He explained that all that evening she kept after him until he felt he had to prove his manhood to her. He didn't even bother to ask her name because he knew he didn't want to see her again.

Simon's condition worsened. Sister Angela increased the dosage of medicine, and changed it, but still he grew weaker by the day. Another distribution was two weeks away, and Father Joe and I were extremely busy so we did not coddle Simon as perhaps we should have. Brother Roland had gone to the Ivory Coast for a short vacation and would be returning a few days before the distribution, so the care of Simon was left to the other three mission boys and one woman, Sarah, who belonged to the same village as Simon. Sarah prepared all kinds of herbal teas for Simon to drink in the hope of curing him, but nothing worked.

One Saturday after Mass, Sister Angela and I went to the hut where the mission boys lived to see how Simon was doing. We were shocked at the sight that confronted us. Simon lay facing the wall curled up in a fetal position. He seemed to be only semiconscious and refused to turn from the wall when we spoke to him. Sister and I prayed with him and left, dismayed at what we had just witnessed. Thankfully, Brother Roland returned that night and immediately devoted all his attention to Simon's care. When he realized how far gone Simon was, he immediately sought those who could help him obtain medicine from the now abandoned hospital. He was able to locate one of the nurses from the hospital who obtained an IV bag which he quickly took to the mission and hooked up to Simon.

That Monday commenced another week of distribution of rice on the mission. As the rowdy, disorderly mob descended on and swiftly filled every space on the campus, we had no choice but to begin the operation. The mood of the students and various teams was very somber. The usual jovial, lighthearted spirit was missing. When we gathered and offered our prayers before the distribution, no one asked for a successful distribution as they normally did. Everyone voiced one plea to God-please let Simon recover completely. But he never did. He remained unconscious throughout the day.

The junior school was still in session so Sister Doris was in her classroom. At the end of the day, when distribution had ended for that day, she and I walked over to visit Simon. He lay on a bed in the priest's house, the IV tube in his arm; another was inserted through his nostril down to his stomach, the other end of which was placed in a bucket at the side of the bed. I became extremely upset when I saw him in that state and I ran out of the room. Sister Doris joined me a few minutes later and we walked home in silence, both fearing that Simon would not last the night.

The next day another area was to be served rice, so Sister and I left the convent before 6:00 A.M. to begin our trek to the mission. When we arrived there about an hour later people were already gathered to collect their rations, but I ignored them while Sister and I hurried over to the mission house, dreading to receive the news. Simon was still in an unconscious state and the bucket at the side of the bed was over half full of a black, foul-smelling substance. I could smell death in the room but I steeled myself and stayed long enough to join Sister as she began to pray the rosary.

Simon's breathing suddenly became erratic. His eyes, which had been tightly shut, flew open and rolled around in his head. Both Father Joe and Brother Roland had gone to the logging companies to obtain fuel and trucks so we did not know what to do. The crowd now gathered at the mission was growing impatient, but I felt unprepared to do anything for them. My whole heart went out to Simon and I felt weak and helpless. I knew he was dying and couldn't bare to just stand by and watch him breathe his last. Sister Doris whispered to me that I should go and pacify the crowd and she would stay with Simon. I all but ran to my office, shut the door, and collapse in the armchair in the corner of the room.

After a few minutes there was a gentle knock and in walked a waif-like ten-year-old whom I had "adopted." Stanley always hung around the mission, hungry, naked, and pitifully thin. His hair was straight and longer than most of the other children's, and his complexion was lighter than most Liberians, leading me to believe that he was of mixed blood. The children teasingly called him "Indian Boy" because he did indeed look like an Indian. After a few months at the mission my students began to refer to him as my son. He was terrified of me at first but began to draw closer and did little things like sweeping the corridor, watering the flowers I had planted all around the school, and other small chores.

One day I called him into my office and asked him if he had ever been to school. Surprisingly, when the child opened his mouth to speak he spoke proper English. He said that he had never been to school but would like to attend even though his mother had no money even to buy food so she couldn't pay his fees. I asked his name and his age, to which he replied that everyone called him "Indian Boy" so that was his name and from what his mother told him, he should be around seven years old. There was a certain street savvy about that child enhanced by a degree of intelligence that I admired. He had an old soul. I looked deep in his eyes and saw that he had suffered much but also knew much. I decided at that moment that he was going to become my protégé.

I cleaned him up, clothed him, sent him to Sister Doris's catechism class and when he was baptized he was promptly named Stanley. Next I had him enrolled in the kindergarten class and he began making great strides as he explored the realms of learning. In return he swept my office, filled a pail of water, and did other small odd jobs. Then he partook of a meal I would prepare and set aside in my office for him. Stanley soon became my shadow. Often the two of us could be seen walking to town, he with my handbag on his shoulder, me holding the basket for the fish, vegetables and other foods we went to purchase.

When he walked into my office that fateful day and saw me curled up crying in the armchair he said nothing but took one look at me and walked out. He returned a few minutes later with a plate in his hand. There was a cupboard in my office where I kept a store of various foodstuff like coffee, sugar, powdered milk, and tinned meat, as well as a flask which he always made sure contained hot water. Silently he set the plate down and proceeded to make a cup of coffee. Even in my tears I marveled at the courage of that little boy. Most people were afraid of me and would not dare to approach me when they saw I was upset. But that ten-year-old broke all barriers. He knew that I cared deeply for him and would never hurt him. Truth was, I knew he guarded me with his life and had become aware of my every whim, even though I hid them from others.

Stanley brought the plate and cup of coffee over to where I sat and urged me to eat. I had to smile, but I was deeply touched by his kindness. I straightened up and invited him to join me. On lifting the cover over the plate I saw that it contained fried ripe plantains, something I loved to eat. So together we devoured the contents and shared the cup of coffee. After that I felt strengthened and realized how hungry I really was. My spirits were lightened even though the sadness of Simon's condition lingered on. Father and Brother returned shortly after and we began the distribution. I had to constantly urge the students to pick up the slack and work with zeal so that we could finish soon. Everyone was disheartened. Even the girls who prepared

177

the meal lacked their usual fervor and the food did not have its usual sweetness.

Around two o'clock in the afternoon Sister Doris summoned me, and when I went over to the house and looked at Simon I knew the end was near. Sister sat holding his hand and praying the rosary. Simon's whole body was convulsing. I had seen many dead, sisters as well as residents of a hospice the sisters were in charge of at home, even helping to wash and dress the bodies, but I had never witnessed anyone actually dying. I could not bear to watch, so I quickly took my leave and once again sought refuge in my office. I had barely closed the door and sat down when there was an urgent knock. When I went to answer, there stood one of the twelfth grade students. I had only to look in his eyes and I knew. I warned him not to say anything to create alarm or panic.

Thousands of people were gathered at the mission. I went into the room where the students were preparing to resume distribution and gathered them around me. I gently broke the news that Simon had passed away and begged them not to scream, but I was too late. Someone had broken the news to the girls gathered at the back of the house and they broke out wailing. Soon everyone caught on and there was widespread wailing and their particular cries of death. I immediately announced that there would be no more distribution for the rest of the day, and as the people slowly left the campus we turned our attention to preparing for Simon's burial.

He was laid to rest a few days later and I was not surprised in the least when I heard it proclaimed that he had been "poisoned" by an irate woman whom he would not allow to cheat. Liberians never believed that someone died of natural causes, especially when so young. In an effort to prove this witchcraft, a well-known "medicine man" was summoned. He "called up" Simon's spirit to name the person who had "poisoned" him. Someone was named, and when investigated it was discovered that Simon had in fact scolded her for cheating, upon which she threatened to "get him." She left the city soon after he became ill and her whereabouts remained unknown.

Under such unfortunate circumstances we were obligated to complete the distribution, otherwise we would have had a riot on our hands. When the last town was served I thought I could breathe a sigh of relief but relief soon turned to dismay when we received word that another ship was arriving in two weeks with enough supplies for the villages on the outskirts. We immediately set about organizing teams and preparing to conduct a census of each of those villages. We zoned off the areas and then chose persons whom we really trusted to lead teams into particular zones. Both Brother Roland and I selected certain areas and led teams there. For us to get to some of those areas we traveled by logging trucks, tractor, canoe, bicycle, and even on foot for miles.

I greatly enjoyed the peace and utter simplicity of the lifestyle of those villages. I was not in the least bit inconvenienced by the lack of modern amenities and luxuries most of us take for granted. There I learned to appreciate the lukewarm bucket baths taken before dawn broke or long after dusk fell. That was because the bathroom was a makeshift structure in a corner of the backyard with neither roof nor door with a matching roughly constructed outdoor toilet house. I rather admired and enjoyed the camaraderie, open friendliness, and simplicity of the villagers who readily accepted strangers into their midst. The houses in these villages varied to include mud-walled huts covered with dried palm branches, zinc and wooded structures, and a few concrete brick houses complete with roofs and awnings.

As we traveled from village to village, whenever we reached a concrete house complete with "palavar" house on the courtyard, we knew we had arrived at the home of the chief of the village. A "palavar" hut is a round hut built of mud, wood or concrete and covered with either palm branches or zinc. In the villages a hut of that kind was used as a community center, court-

179

house or recreation center and that was why it was constructed on the property of the chief or close to his home. Very often my team and I were accommodated in the house of the chief from where we conducted the census and, later distributed the food.

Even though I went to distribute food, I was prepared for any emergency, so I took a good supply of medicine. I always took a flask of hot water and a jar of coffee because, depending on the situation, I could survive on coffee. The interior villages were usually extremely cold so I always carried enough blankets for the members of my team and me. One day when I was departing for a particularly dangerous village deep in the forest, Brother Roland came to bid me good-bye. He surveyed the mountain of stuff I was taking and asked me two questions: "Sister, you going?" "Yes, Brother, I am going," I replied as we embraced and hugged each other. "Sister, you coming back?" Brother then asked which made everyone gathered around burst into peals of laughter.

In the evenings, after a very tiring day of distributing the supplies to the endless lines of villagers, I looked forward to going off for a long walk or just be alone with nature, but the villagers would have none of that. While I was there I belonged to them, so they constantly sought my attention. I spent hours cleaning, disinfecting, and bandaging cuts, gunshot wounds, and even snake bites. I counseled young and old who sought my advise on various matters which included domestic squabbles, pregnant twelve and thirteen-year-olds; baptizing newborn babies or telling stories to those who would just come to sit with me and chat. Although I felt cheated out of the solitude and rest I so badly needed and yearned for, I was deeply touched and often felt that was exactly how Jesus spent his time when he began his ministry. Swamped and enveloped by those poor, hungry, weak, and wounded men, women, and children made me realize the awesome presence of Jesus in our midst. I was tremendously humbled by that realization and made every attempt to bring those gathered around me closer to him.

Very often I performed tasks that made my stomach lurch so violently I thought it was going to be ripped out. One day as I walked through a village I came upon a little girl whose teeth and gums were in a severe state of decay. I spoke to her asking if her mouth hurt but she wouldn't answer me. I told the mother that I would like to attend to her and she gave me permission to do so. I sat on a bench and placed the child on my lap, then I began to administer a treatment I had seen Sister Angela perform in the clinic.

I poured a drop of gentian violet from the bottle I always carried into a bowl of water and with Q-tips I gently and patiently cleaned the inside of the girl's mouth. The smell made me want to vomit, but I held my mouth tightly shut and swallowed constantly to keep down the bile. I had tied my hair up in a ponytail and did not wear my veil so that the villagers would feel more comfortable. While I cleaned the child's mouth she did not pay the least attention to what I was doing because she became fascinated with my hair. She pulled the tresses over my shoulder to the front and kept running her fingers through them. I knew that the ministrations performed on her mouth, gentle though they were, must have hurt her, but not once did she cry out or even wince. When I was done I hugged and praised her for being so brave. She slid off my lap and ran to the mother declaring in the dialect of the village, "Mumah, uh numoh gieh!" I was alarmed, thinking that I had hurt her, but her mother smiled and patted my hand as she assured me, "My daughter says you are beautiful."

In another village I was taken to visit a woman who was shot through her stomach by the rebels as she ran for safety into the forest. Her whole family had gathered in her house expecting her to die at any time. With no formal training in nursing, being confronted with a medical problem of that size and nature made me inwardly cry out to God for courage, strength, and a good old miracle! As I entered the house, everyone turned and looked at me trustingly, expecting me to do just that -- perform a miracle to save that woman!

My stomach recoiled at the stench emanating from the body on the bed. I gulped and swallowed as I approached the woman writhing and crying out in pain. I patted her hand and whispered to her to be still for a moment so I could look at the wound. I gently and carefully removed the layers of covers that were placed on top of her and then I unwrapped the wound. There appeared what looked like a half-inch hole that seemed to have penetrated straight through to her back. I unpacked the bag of medicines I carried and began to disinfect the wound and the area around it. I felt utterly helpless because all I really had were pain killers and some antibiotics.

I hastily uttered a prayer and did something I had seen my mother do some years back to cure a sore in an old man's foot. I asked for a clean piece of cloth and a bottle or stone. I placed some of the tablets in the cloth and proceeded to grind them into a powder with the bottle. When I had achieved a fine enough powder, I packed it firmly into the hole and covered it over with a clean piece of gauze. I then gave her two of the antibiotics to drink and left the balance with her daughter to administer later on. I spoke encouraging words to the woman and her family and hastily retreated from the room not wanting the threatening tears to spill over.

CHAPTER TEN

Problems continually beset us as we proceeded with the rice distributions throughout the entire county of Sinoe. In the city, we were constantly confronted with issues such as the lack of fuel and trucks to transport the rice, the unwillingness of drivers to travel into some of the villages in the interior of the forest, the growing harassment by the rebels to seize the supplies, and worst of all large scale theft and misappropriation of the supplies by team leaders and members. I began to feel more like a magistrate than an administrator as I was constantly having to punish those caught stealing the rice, selling it, or exchanging it for favors. When I demoted or dismissed those whom I caught, I garnered their anger and hatred. I was quite fearless and unafraid for myself, but concerned for the members of my team especially one young man, Clint.

I first laid eyes on Clint in 1990 when he accompanied the mission boys Simon and Robert to my office. They had come to plead for permission to use the newly reconstructed school auditorium to host a dance. When I saw the tall young man with the full afro hairstyle walk into my office I could only stare, not listening to what any of the others had to say. I stared in disbelief. There indeed before me was the young man I had dreamed exactly twenty years before, in 1970, when my country had experienced civil unrest. That was the young man who had rescued my mother and me from the mob in which we were caught. I uttered not a word to him but saw him frequently after, since he became a student of the Bible School.

He was way past the age for high school and had in fact graduated a few years before. His dream was to attend the university in Monrovia, but his parents could not afford to pay the fees so he hung around. Instead of continuing to stay at home and waste time, when we opened the school, he registered and began attending classes, but not for long. Sister Doris was seeking assistance with the kindergarten class and asked if I had anyone interested and capable of being an assistant teacher. When I inquired, Clint volunteered, and she could not have been more pleased with his performance.

At the very beginning of the rice distribution Clint got involved in a massive conspiracy, was wrongfully accused, and was imprisoned. I was not aware of all that transpired but got wind of it only when Father and Brother summoned everyone involved in the distribution to attend a meeting on the campus. When I heard what had supposedly happened, I was indeed shocked but I decided to take Clint under my wing from that day forward. He became a member of my team, and as I worked closely with him I grew to understand why Father and Brother loved, trusted, and respected him so much and why everyone around, including his family members and friends, were consumed with hatred and jealousy.

There was great potential in that young man. He was extremely kind-hearted, remarkably loving and lovable, which made him quite a charmer among the ladies, young and not so young, but he was nevertheless conscientious, responsible, and dependable. Recognizing those qualities and his commitment to wiping out dishonesty in the distribution process, Father Joseph chose Clint and another young man, Nat, who was the son of the city magistrate, to visit homes where we suspected there were incidents of fraud. Those two young men were greatly instrumental in rooting out major fraud and cases of corruption, but my fears and concerns grew, especially for Clint, who was constantly being threatened. Every discovery of dishonesty brought added threats and intimidation.

Instead of discouraging him or taking away the task entrusted to him, Father Joe, Brother, and I encouraged him and Nat to have courage and strength. I prayed unceasingly that the angels would protect Clint. Others who were entrusted with distributing the rice and had keys to the warehouse outside of the campus where it was stored, openly stole the rice. They devised plans, they stole the rice, hid it, and then proceeded to blame Clint for putting the stolen rice to his own use. While everyone else pointed fingers at him, Father Brother and I remained firm in our conviction of his innocence. He lived near the campus and was very friendly with Father and Brother, so he was almost always hanging out on the mission. Often they would recall nights when they played Scrabble until the wee hours of the morning. Brother would exclaim, "Sister, that boy can cheat-O, that's why he always win!" Not content with being beaten, Father and Brother encouraged him to continue playing so that they could attain victory. In that way, they knew where he was when the rice was being stolen and that he could not have been responsible.

Tension grew, and the jealousy, threats, lies, and even physical rage became almost unbearable. In the midst of that turmoil I had to leave Greenville for a few weeks to attend a seminar in Cape Palmas. I was loathe to leave Clint to those who sought to harm him, but both Father and Brother assured me they would make sure that no harm would befall him. I was well aware of the extent to which Liberians went to seek revenge on their enemies, even their own flesh and blood, and not entirely ignorant of the ways they "protected" themselves from the evil of others.

Parents sought to "protect" their child from evil the minute he or she was born. Certain rituals were performed on a newborn and certain marks were made on the body with a fresh, unused razor. The size, shape, and so on of the mark signified the particular tribe of the child but it was also used for another purpose. Those cuts were rubbed or filled with various herbs and other elements in order to concoct their special protective "medicine." Adults also used other ways of "protecting" themselves from evil. I asked Clint if he participated in any such practices and he assured me that he didn't, but he admitted that he had great strength and no fear of evil, and he was sure it was because of whatever his parents did to his body when he was born. I nevertheless urged him to be careful and to pray unceasingly while I was gone.

When I returned to Greenville after the two weeks I had to be off again. I had volunteered to visit all the Catholic schools in the diocese. That entailed driving into towns and villages that had not been entered since they were attacked by the rebels, so no one knew what to expect. I decided to take Clint on that journey with me. I thought it would be a learning experience for him and take him away from the tension he constantly faced in the city. I was glad I did because on our return there was a full-blown investigation into more theft of rice and to my astonishment and consternation people were actually accusing Clint, even saying that they saw him carrying sacks of rice to his home in the night! I was angry but then the whole thing seemed so funny. Unless he was a magician, how could he have been in two places at the same time? I made up my mind to erase the animosity, hatred, and jealousy for Clint.

Meanwhile, another ship arrived in our port laden with supplies. That was February 1992. Once again I cleared it with customs and secured additional storage space in warehouses around town for the supplies, which were about five times more than we could store in the school. Once again, Brother, Father, and I made the rounds of the seven logging companies in Greenville procuring fuel and trucks to transport the rice throughout the county. Each time Father or Brother had to approach one of the managers, they asked me to accompany them. I agreed, naively thinking that it was because they enjoyed my company. Later I discovered that I was being used as "bait."

Unknown to me, all the men in charge of the logging companies had taken a fancy to me and readily granted favors to Father and Brother when I was present. I couldn't understand how or why they became attracted to me because I never fraternized with them nor encouraged them. I knew them all and was very polite and sweet whenever we met, but that was as far as it went. As nuns, we frequently experienced men falling at our feet, wanting to do our every bidding. Some of my friends back home would tell me that the nuns had a certain aura that mystified men and caused them to want to "discover" us. I knew some sisters who used that to their advantage in order to help others less fortunate. Now, there I was, faced with the same situation, so without hurting anyone or becoming involved illicitly, I would use my charms and good looks to gain the assistance we so desperately needed.

The distribution that followed was extremely successful. We reached thousands of people hidden in villages beyond the city and in every nook and cranny of the forest. Again we were faced with immense problems, mainly from the rebels who kept arriving in droves every day and threatening to take away all the supplies to feed themselves. I fought relentlessly for a fair and just dispensation of the rice, beans, corn meal, and used clothing. Except for the few grumblers and theft, people were generally satisfied and happy with what they received.

At the end of the operation I left for my long-awaited and much-needed vacation. I spent two months in England but constantly missed my work, the students and the few friends I had made in Liberia, especially Clint. I did a week's retreat during which I did a lot of praying, meditating, and self-searching, and at the conclusion made a few decisions that would determine the path my life would take upon returning to Liberia. I was taken to visit the various convents the order had in England. The sisters subjected me to long interrogations about the people and the general situation, but I constantly felt that no one really cared about me or even the other sisters. They just wanted "news" to further build their case about our mission in Liberia.

When the mission was announced, many of the sisters were dead set against it, but their reasons were all selfish and prejudiced. Every opportunity they got, the more aggressive ones tried to dissuade those of us chosen to go to Liberia from going.

In England, my disgust and aversion for the nuns grew. Some of them existed in their own make-believe world, depending on the security and luxury of convent life. Some of those nuns who had professed a vow of poverty lived lavish lifestyles. They hadn't the faintest idea of poverty because they shut themselves away from the challenges of the real world out there. All the sisters in England were busy getting "their" work done so I ended up leaving earlier than I had planned. I went directly to Monrovia where I stayed with some friends of Clint before returning to Greenville.

CHAPTER ELEVEN

On my return to Greenville I discovered a new pastor who was also the vicar general of the diocese. Father Joe was recalled to Cape Palmas and Brother Roland had rejoined his community who had returned to Monrovia. There was not a grain of rice left in the school. That pleased me because I no longer wanted to be involved with the distributions. I wanted to clean up the school, replant the front courtyard with the shrubs and flowers that had been destroyed during the distributions, and get on with the business of running the school and educating the students.

Father Martin was a very amiable and extremely intelligent man but he came to Greenville with bitterness and unfriendliness and remained aloof. He felt that he was being punished by the bishop. Anytime a priest was sent to Greenville, he regarded the assignment as a punishment by the bishop because Greenville was so remote and not as modern as the other towns. The people there were backward because they held on to their old ways, and almost all the young men and women left immediately for Monrovia upon graduating from high school.

The very first thing I did when I opened my office door on my return from England was to remove a cupboard with all the rice records and place it in the mission house. I did not care who looked after the operation or what they did, but I was not going to be involved anymore and neither would I allow the school to be used. I then spent the month of August reconstructing and refurbishing the school to resume classes in September. I had received numerous donations of books from England and those were used to expand our library. I applied to foreign agencies to procure funds to build a library and house a typing class, and one agency supplied funds for the typing school. I was thus able to purchase over twenty typewriters and a copying machine. When I advertised the beginning of the typing class the response was overwhelming. Not only did the entire senior class register, so did a lot of adults. The fee was five dollars a month, but those who absolutely couldn't afford it weren't denied the opportunity to learn to type. They simply performed some chore around the campus in return for their hour's tuition.

There were close to one hundred students in the high school and over two hundred in the junior school. Sister Doris had a new principal, Laura, who had been the principal of a school run by nuns in another town. When the nuns left they asked us to employ her. Sister was quite pleased with her. I had lured some of the finest teachers in the city to join the staff of the high school. We had an exceptional science teacher whom I chose as the vice-principal. Students still could not afford to pay the original fees of our school, so after holding meetings we decided on a fair amount that everyone would be able to afford. Then the diocese announced that it had received funds to award scholarship grants to a certain number of students in each school. What we received there plus the money we received from fees was used to pay the teachers a substantial salary. We soon learned that our teachers were the only people in the town actually receiving a salary, so every day we received requests to hire more teachers but I held fast to the number I had.

Again special projects were organized to enthuse the students to learn and to give their all. I drew up a large chart of progress and posted it outside my office. Teachers were encouraged to give quizzes as often as possible and those grades were handed in to me. At the end of each week they were tallied up and the students with the highest marks in each subject had their name written on a gold, silver, blue or red star and stuck on the chart in order of merit. It is a known fact that everyone loves to see their name written up in public and my students were no exception. Every Friday afternoon as the bell rang for dismissal, they would all flock around the chart to see if their name had made it.

At the end of the month prizes were awarded to the students with the top scores, and a special prize was conferred upon the student with the highest grade point average in the whole school. Surprisingly, that position of top overall student was won and steadily held by a student of the tenth grade who was exceptionally brilliant. It soon became obvious that such positive reinforcement like the posting up of names and awarding prizes served as a means of helping the students to rebuild their shattered lives, stimulating their self-confidence, restoring their dignity, and cultivating a sense of care and concern not only for themselves but for their fellow school mates.

With Father Martin at the mission, I was not obligated to, but out of courtesy invited him to teach religion and take an interest in the school. He readily accepted, but fell into the routine of coming to the building, teaching his class, and returning to his house. Gone was the friendliness shared between the sisters and the former pastors. Gone was the camaraderie I had shared with Father Joe and Brother Roland, who never sat down to a meal without sending a student to call me once I was on the mission.

I missed that but I missed more than ever the friendship of Father Joe and Brother Roland. There were times when Father Martin seemed rather desolate and lonely, but I stayed at a distance. He had isolated himself by his aloofness and arrogance and I was not about to go beyond my call of duty and inquire what ailed him as I would normally have done. Not long after he was joined on the mission by a newly ordained priest, Father Alex. He was very effervescent and outgoing, and the young people all thronged around him.

At that particular time the sisters were in dire need of foodstuff and medicine and there was no way for us to obtain those things except to either travel to the Ivory Coast or to Monrovia. After asking around I learned that Joseph, a Lebanese shopkeeper who had not abandoned Greenville during the war, was planning to journey to Monrovia to purchase a new truck. Joseph was going in his Pajero jeep and was taking two persons, which meant that he had room for two others. Clint had previously spoken of the need to travel to Monrovia to search for important documents which he had left in his grandfather's house where he had been living before the war, so I asked Joseph to take us both.

On our journey to Monrovia we constantly encountered erratic, drunken, and harassing rebels at the numerous checkpoints but Joseph kept them at bay by handing out fistfuls of money. As we approached a town called Karisburg, Joseph asked what kind of money we were carrying. Under normal circumstances that would have sounded like a strange question but then it made much sense. Liberia had been split into two completely separate sections, much like two separate countries. There was a distinct line of demarcation between Monrovia and the "rest" of Liberia. To be able to drive in Monrovia, you had to have a different driver's license, and to be caught carrying the old "JJ," the money used in the rest of Liberia, was grounds for severe punishment.

Sister Doris had suggested that I make a money belt out of cloth to be worn under my habit, and that's where I stashed the money I was carrying. I just prayed hard that none of the rebels would dare to strip or body search me. I did have some "JJs" with me, but they were hidden in the deep pocket of my habit which was hidden by the many folds in the cloth. I had forgotten to ask Clint what he carrying, and by the time I turned around to ask him I saw the pile of old dollars in his hand. He quickly tried to hide it in the jeep but was not swift enough. The rebels were approaching so he panicked and stuck it in his pocket. Big mistake!

All the men were roughly requested to disembark and go to the office to be searched. The rebels looked me up and down and told me to remain in the jeep. I obeyed but I was apprehensive about what would happen once the old dollars were found on Clint. I did not have to wait long to find out. Joseph came back to tell me that they were indeed found on Clint and he was taken to another room and locked up for interrogation. I felt my whole body grow cold. I knew what the rebels did to those whom they "held for interrogation." I immediately disembarked and went to the office. I was terribly afraid and held my rosary beads tightly for strength.

Joseph pointed to the door of the room where Clint had been taken and I approached it trembling. I imagined him being tied up and even severely beaten, the treatment meted out to men and even women in that situation. I knocked gently and opened the door. My eyes scanned the room for Clint, and I was relieved to see him fully dressed and unharmed. He sat on a bench and looked like a lost, terrified little boy.

At that moment I felt an outpouring of incomparable, unconditional love for Clint and a strong desire to protect him. I realized that I approached my destiny. Clint was my destiny, and I was destined to love him. I had known that when I first met him but I kept ignoring it. I shouldn't love him the way I did, my religious life did not permit that, but somehow that did not matter then. Common sense told me that my emotions were dangerous folly, but what I felt for Clint was too strong, too compelling, and I refused to listen to the voice of reason.

When I entered the room I politely greeted everyone and inquired what was wrong. One rebel, who identified himself as the commanding officer, replied that this young man was violating the law so had to be detained in jail and punished. I asked what his crime was and the rebel replied that Clint had unacceptable money that had to be confiscated and, besides, he "looked suspicious." Around that time there were rumors of the emergence of another warring faction, the ULIMO forces, and there were many stories of brutalities committed by the rebels against young male travelers whom they suspected to be ULIMO supporters. There I was surrounded by a band of erratic, unreasonable, unintelligent men posing as "soldiers," and I had to convince them that the young man who faced their wrath was neither soldier nor rebel. I used my wits to think of something quickly enough to appease them.

"I am ever so sorry that we are carrying the currency used in our region," I explained as I removed the stack of money I carried in my pocket and handed it over, "but we were not aware of the rule. This is the first time we are traveling to Monrovia and we were going to purchase foodstuff for the sisters and medicine for the clinic. Here, please take what I have too, and pardon us." I guess I was pushing fate and my luck as well, but my reasoning was that, technically, if I carried the old "JJs" I should also be punished, but I knew they dared not strip or beat me because then they would have Archbishop Mike and the whole church to deal with.

"Okay, Sister, you win that one but we still have to search him for special marks because we suspect him to be a ULIMO soldier," the commander countered. "Well, you can search him but I can tell you now, he is not involved in either politics or military actions. He works in the school with the sisters and is very active in the church and the community, so please save yourselves the trouble, forgive us, and let us go in peace." I pleaded. If the need had arisen for me to get on my knees I would have done so.

Convent life offered countless occasions of humiliation and chances to humble oneself, but never in the ten years I had spent behind the convent walls had I been so humiliated. The rebels' eyes bored through me as I stood there, humbling myself and pleading for the life of that young man who had become so very important to me. Finally, the commander waved his hand toward Clint as an indication for him to go, and we all but ran out of the room after thanking them profusely. When we got to the jeep and Joseph drove off I turned around to the back seat, glared at Clint, and scolded him for not being more careful. I was scared to death and would certainly faint from fear and exhaustion if we had to go through that experience again.

Once we arrived in Monrovia Joseph drove to the home of Clint's relatives where we were to stay then proceeded to find his wife and his newborn with whom he was looking forward to being reunited. The baby girl had been born during the war, and Joseph had immediately sent her and his wife to stay with relatives in Monrovia so he hadn't seen them in ages. Clint was afraid for me to venture out, so while I stayed indoors he did the shopping. After a few days word came that the situation had worsened in our region of the country. We sought out Joseph to tell him and ask him if we could return as soon as possible. When we got to his wife's home, we found him on his sick bed. He had succumbed to a terrible attack of malaria and could not even hold up his head. We therefore had to seek other means to return to Greenville.

We returned to the place where we were staying, packed our bags, bid a hasty farewell to everyone, and hit the road to find a taxi to take us to an area called "Red Light." If we were in luck we could hire another one to take us from there to Greenville, but I dreaded to think of the sum they would demand. There were literally hundreds of people at the "Red Light" area searching for taxis or trucks to take them to Greenville. We saw a lot of people we knew, but I had to pretend I didn't know them when they came up and greeted us in an over friendly manner. I knew just what would happen. The moment I got a taxi, they would jump in and I would have to pay for them! Their hopes would be dashed, however, because I was not going to fall prey to their ruse.

After waiting for over an hour, we were able to procure seats in a taxi going as far as Gbarnga. Gbarnga was a large town just on the outskirts of Monrovia, and it was where Ray Harper, the leader of the NPFL, had established his headquarters. In the back seat of the taxi sat three women, one with a baby, and a young man who was the son of one of the women. That left the front seat free, so Clint and I jumped in. We were charged fifty dollars each but I didn't mind - I just wanted to get out of there.

As the driver drove off, though, I knew we were in for trouble. He proclaimed that he had been a driver for Samuel Doe and he was going to get even with those "dirty, pissing tail" rebels who harassed him!

At the first major checkpoint, the rebels requested the driver's license. He declared that he didn't have one, but proudly presented his ID from the Doe regime. I wanted to punch the man in his face. At that time, everyone and their dogs knew how much the rebels hated Doe, whom they had captured and murdered, and any form of life associated with him. So, of course, the rebels began to rejoice because they smelled blood. They demanded that everyone "fall down" (that was the term they used to tell people who were traveling to disembark from their vehicle). The driver was roughly hauled from the car, handcuffed, and thrown into a cell, while the rebels gleefully said that there would be an execution right there.

My skin began to crawl and my stomach froze because I knew the rebels were capable of shooting the man in cold blood in front of all of us. They began jumping up and down while firing their weapons in the air. I could see the other travelers grow apprehensive and decided to take matters in my hands. I warned Clint to shut up and remain still while I approached the table where a few rebels were seated. I greeted them politely and asked to see their commander. A young man wearing a blond wig identified himself as the leader, and I addressed myself to him. I pleaded for him to let the driver go so that we could continue our journey. While I spoke I stared him straight in his eyes and did not once waver or avert my eyes. He stared back for a few seconds and finally asked, "How much you willing to pay, 'ooman?" I took out twenty dollars from my pocket and gave it to him, saying that that was all I had. He snatched the money out of my hands and yelled for his men to bring the driver out.

When we returned to the car, instead of the driver being thankful that his life had been spared, the stupid man began to argue with the soldiers. I shouted to him to shut up and drive his car. As we drove off, Clint began to reprimand him, but the arrogant fool began to argue and boast that the soldiers would never have killed him. I was so mad. I told him to stop the car and refund our money and we would walk the rest of the way. He knew that he would not get that kind of money again, so he continued arguing. I told Clint to shut up and ignore him so that he would eventually shut up too.

At the checkpoint indicating the entrance into Gbarnga, we again had to disembark. The men were taken to one room while the women were taken to another by a very pregnant female rebel. She had her face painted with the traditional war marks and her mouth was covered with a strange smelling white powder. She embraced me and kissed me on my cheek declaring ever so sweetly, "How you do Mamie?" and in the same breath her countenance turned beastly as she pointed her gun, roughly greeted the women, and announced, "You better strip down, today I goin' see your butts!"

I could see the fear in their eyes because I suspected they were carrying large sums of money as I was so, if we were stripped and searched not only would our money be taken away but we would also be severely punished. One of the women pleaded that she was menstruating while I humbly added that we were innocent women so there was no need to harass or humiliate us. While saying that I placed twenty dollars in her hand. Again she embraced and kissed me and declared, "Thank you, thank you, Mamie, you do well!" Then turning to the women she savagely declared, "You people lucky-O, the Mamie save you, but next time I goin' catch your tails!"

When we got into Gbarnga the driver deposited us at the "packing" station and we were left on our own. At the depot we met the two young men who had traveled with Joseph to Monrovia. They too had somehow managed to obtain rides as far as Gbarnga. They immediately latched themselves onto us, and I knew it was only because they felt that I would obtain rides for them to Greenville. I was too tired to bother, so I let them follow us as we picked up our bags and headed for the Catholic mission. When we arrived there, the place seemed desolate and deserted. That was the well-kept, lavish mission I had visited when I had first arrived in Liberia to attend the seminar for all new missionaries. There was grass as tall as I growing all around the buildings. We stopped at the bishop's house and looked around. Clint called out and a young man appeared from the backyard. We asked for the bishop and he replied that Bishop Dotu had left the mission, but one sister was there in the convent. I thanked him and approached the convent.

Sister Mary greeted us like old friends even though I had never laid eyes on her before. We explained our plight and after settling me into the convent, she retrieved the keys for the guest house and settled the three young men in rooms there. After taking a luxurious, hot shower I joined the boys for a meal, then they decided to walk into the city to search for anything on four wheels traveling to Greenville. They returned late that night having spent a fruitless evening but promised to return the next day and the next for as long as it took them to obtain a lift to Greenville for us. Two days later we got word that a pickup belonging to one of the logging companies would be passing through. That driver had taken my team and me to the village where I had treated the woman with the gunshot wound, so we were sure he would find room for the four of us.

Two evenings later, having paid one hundred dollars for each of the two young men I had inherited, plus Clint and myself, we were on our way to Greenville. I shared the front seat with the driver and another man who apparently was traveling with the payroll for the workers of the logging company. He kept the bag with the money hidden under the seat but when I entered the vehicle he pushed it over under my feet. Each time we arrived at a checkpoint and they had to descend I was told to remain in the vehicle, and therefore the bag of money was safe under my feet. At the crack of dawn we arrived in Greenville to face whatever was happening there.

The school progressed slowly but surely. In my absence Sister Doris had held down the fort and kept both the junior and senior classes functioning. We still continued to be extremely careful of everything we said and did. Frequently new groups of rebels arrived in Greenville and immediately set about beating up and humiliating the ones they met, as well as harassing civilians. In an effort to demobilize the rebels, a peacekeeping force, ECOMOG, was sent to Liberia. ECOMOG was the name given to a conglomeration of soldiers from most of the West African countries.

Ray Harper hated them with a passion. He called them by every name in the book and encouraged hostility between his band of rebels and the peacekeeping soldiers. They had been concentrating only on Monrovia but they had begun infiltrating the other areas of Liberia. Surprising as it may sound, their presence stirred up renewed fighting. That was because even though they were not supposed to use force or violence to retaliate against rebel attacks, they did. When they arrived in Greenville they were met with animosity from the rebels, but that was spurred by their cruelty to the rebels. Rebels were supposed to turn in their weapons to the ECOMOG soldiers and be guaranteed safety but often they were executed. So they preferred to run away with their weapons.

The soldiers then had the run of the city. They harassed civilians, took away properties, vehicles, and anything they could lay their hands on, even the women who had become the girlfriends of the rebels. After a few weeks in hiding, the rebels gathered forces, collected ammunition, crept into town in the middle of the night and raided the soldiers' headquarters. They stripped the soldiers, donned their uniforms, tied them up, and stole all their food, money, and goods that had been stashed in the headquarters. Complete bedlam ruled. The rebels further humiliated the soldiers by dressing them in women's clothing, bundling them in a truck, and sending them back to Monrovia. Everyone felt that the soldiers would seek revenge, but no one knew nor could imagine how, and so they caught the city by surprise when they did.

After the soldiers left Greenville in disgrace, things were too quiet to be real. The air was tense, but no one knew what to expect. We did not have to wait long to find out. One Sunday, about a month later, Sisters Angela, Doris, and I were inside the convent when we heard the distant droning of jets. Sister Doris recognized and identified the sound as that of fighter jets. As we rushed out the front door and into the yard, the sounds grew closer and louder. We looked up into the sky and saw five jets flying around in circles. They seemed to be staking out the convent and flew low enough for us to see the soldiers sitting in them armed with machine guns. Suddenly one of the jets dipped its nose and seemed to head straight at us.

As we hastily withdrew to the safety of the convent, I ran into the chapel and dropped to my knees. The jets kept circling the convent for about ten minutes, then flew off and dropped a bomb that hit the airfield office building. After that day, there were frequent air raids by the soldiers of the ECOMOG forces. It was reported that they were trying to "flush" out the NPFL rebels, but what no one understood or cared about was that they were killing innocent people in their "cleansing" process. The outside world was being inundated by the news of what a commendable job the forces were doing in keeping the peace in Monrovia but no one was aware of the terror they brought to the rest of the country. Those air raids had come just when some sense of normalcy was returning to Greenville, so they caused panic among all of us living there.

As we got on with our lives, our ears became attuned to the feared sounds of the jets. One day I was in my office in the school when I heard them. I ran out quickly to calm the students and teachers alike. The jets drew near and circled the school for a while. The students threw themselves on the ground or under their desks and waited. I stood on the corridor to make sure no one ran out into the courtyard and risk being shot at. When we heard the jets fly off, some of the students joined me in the corridor and we watched in horror as the port area was bombed. Later that day we learned that the port manager's house, a few other houses around, and part of the port area were destroyed. For a long time after, I kept having nightmares of the bombings, seeing the jets with lights blaring like two large evil eyes, and nose dipped, ready to pounce on their prey. The terrifying sound of the engines accelerated was the hardest to erase from my mind. Soon our school population began to diminish as once again parents began to remove their children and send them to the forest for safety.

In the meantime, my concerns for Clint's safety was growing as jealousy grew. Even the elders in the church felt that he should not be my assistant in the school, in the many areas in which his help was invaluable, that I should not spend so much time tutoring him as I endeavored to prepare him for college. I had begun applying to colleges in the United States in order to obtain a scholarship for him. There was someone with immense potential and I was going to do all in my power to ensure that he amounted to something. As my mother would have said, everyone washed their mouths on us, but I paid no mind to the rumors circulating or the hatred of those responsible. I grasped at every opportunity that presented itself to have Clint leave Greenville. Whenever the sisters or the school needed supplies I sent him to the Ivory Coast or to Monrovia. I missed him dreadfully when he was gone, but I was relieved that he was out of range of those who seemed bent on destroying him.

As the air raids grew worse, people began retreating to the forest in droves. Even the two priests were away for most of the attacks. Both left Greenville in January to attend a seminar in Cape Palmas but remained longer than anticipated, so Sister Angela, Doris and I were completely on our own.

The first Sunday in March brought a particularly harsh attack on the port. Most of the homes were bombed out and the few people who had remained all moved away. The port manager came by with news that the jets or "doo doo boys," as the Liberians called them, would be visiting Greenville again the next Tuesday to finish the job. Most people did not take heed. Right at that time, our passports needed to be renewed and we were advised to turn them in to the Immigration Department. Of course, the "Immigration Department" that existed in Greenville was only a sham. There was no proper government but only rebels making a farce out of law and order.

On Monday morning after settling the students into their various classes, I walked the mile into town to get to the office. I went up the three flights of stairs and presented the three passports to the officer seated behind a large, empty desk. I knew it should be only a matter of having the books stamped and then paying the "fee" required. The rebels in positions of responsibility charged a fee for everything, and I used to remark that they would begin to charge people for sneezing! The surly, foul-looking rebel informed me that the "chief" had left the building with the keys to the desk so the stamp was locked up, but I could leave the passports and return. I was not about to leave our passports with such a character, so I said that I would wait, but after waiting for three hours, I decided to leave.

I was angry and disgusted with the whole situation. I whizzed past the other rooms unaware that I had just passed the courtroom. The judge was an elder in the church and one of the few people I loved and trusted. He was married to Clint's mother's eldest sister, and the two families were extremely close. As I hurried down the stairs, he stood at the top and hollered after me to slow down and come back up. I retraced my steps and went into his office with him.

"What's wrong, Sis, you're as angry like a bull," Vincent gently asked. I quickly told him about our passports and what I had just experienced. I had wasted a whole half-day. He expressed his disgust and comforted me by saying that I should return to school and come back in the afternoon. If after that I still had not gotten the passports stamped, I could leave them with him.

That lifted my spirits and I returned to the school campus. When school was dismissed, Sister Doris accompanied me to the office.

When we got there we were greeted with a "Closed for Lunch" sign on the front door. The woman living next door said that the "officers" would return soon, and offered us a bench to sit and wait. The sun was scorching hot and burned our faces and hands even though we sat in the shade of a tree. "Those officers certainly have long lunch hours!" Sister Doris declared after we had waited for three hours. When the church bells rang the six o'clock Angelus we knew that the men were not going to return for that day. We realized then that our only hope lay in Vincent's offer, so we had to get the passports to him. Wearily we began the two-mile walk back to the convent.

We rose with the sun the next day and set out bright and early at 6:30 A.M. briskly walking the hour-long journey to the school. Sister Doris headed over to the junior school while I opened my office in the senior high. As students arrived, we cheerily greeted them and sent them to their respective class-rooms to do supervised reading. Previously, when students arrived before the bell was rung, they were allowed to run wild and make as much noise as in the market place. Then, when it was time to go to classes, they would be hot, sweaty, and exhausted.

I thought that was ridiculous and thus instituted a new prac-tice. Students were allowed to take a book from the library and sit in their classroom quietly reading until the bell was rung. Usually a teacher or the senior student elected as the prefect of that grade supervised the students. That change brought immense satisfaction for everyone--students got extra time to accrue additional knowledge, teachers did not have to do "yard" duty (which they hated), and we got the peace and quiet that I felt was necessary to begin the day.

Martin and Oliver, the two boys who assisted us in the con-vent, were students in our school, and I anxiously awaited the arrival of either one. When I saw Martin, I called out to him to come to my office. I asked him to kindly run an errand for me and, giving him the passports to take to Vincent's house, I strongly warned him, "Don't you dare give this package to anyone but Mr. Vincent, not even to his shadow!" Martin laughed but he understood and set out for the short walk over to the man's house.

Students were extremely restless that morning, and it took some doing to settle them down at assembly. As they marched into their classrooms I visited each room to make sure that the appointed teacher was there and that the students were ready to begin a new day of learning. I had the tenth grade for religion and always looked forward to that session. The students were extremely intelligent and, as a result, lively discussions always arose on whatever topic I had chosen to teach. I had decided to broach the subject of "The Presence of Evil among Us" that day. As I turned my back to the students and began writing on the chalkboard, my hand froze in midair. I could not believe my ears. There in the distance but drawing closer and closer were the sounds of the fighter jets.

Without warning we seemed to be surrounded by jets bearing soldiers heavily armed and shooting in every direction. Students and teachers alike panicked. I yelled to my students to hit the floor and most of them crawled under their desks. I ran out the door and into the next classroom, yelled the same order to the twelfth graders, and looked around for the teacher. Mr. King, my vice-principal, cowered beneath the teacher's desk, his eyes popping out of their sockets in terror. I ran to him, touched his arm, and told him to stay there, that everything would be okay. I attempted to get the few students there to run across to the next room so everyone could be together but they stared at me and remained rooted to the spot where they stood or lay.

I could hear the terrified screams of the students of the junior school and longed to go over there and comfort them but the only way to get there was to cross the short courtyard that was being littered with bullets. The air attack seemed endless. The jets literally sat over the school roof and pumped bullets around us. I kept walking the corridor, and one of them flew so low I was able to look the soldier directly in his face. I wanted to scream out that we were just innocent children under the care of two harmless nuns, but when I saw him aim his gun at me I ran into the classroom and shut the door. Bullets were fired but they hit the walls and did not reach us inside the room.

The jets suddenly changed direction and headed off for the port area. I ran out on the corridor, and some of the braver students joined me as we watched bombs being dropped over and over on the port. Without warning they again changed course and turned right back in the direction of the school. We quickly scampered back into the classroom, but when they passed over and continued on in the opposite direction, we ran to the windows and watched as bombs were dropped in the direction of the convent. Vincent's daughter held her mouth and exclaimed, "O God, Sister, the convent gone-O!"

I was suddenly chilled to the bone as I thought of Sister Angela and her patients in the clinic. All the time I was tightly grasping my rosary but could not utter a word of prayer, I was so confused and scared. But, just holding fast to it gave me courage and strength. Those teachers who had been preparing their lessons in the teachers' lounge had joined the students gathered in the tenth grade classroom. It was a pitiful sight to see students and teachers alike cowering in fear during that vicious attack by the ECOMOG soldiers. They continued to randomly bomb different sections of the city, then fly back to circle the mission and discharge several rounds of bullets. I awaited the bomb which was inevitable but it never came. The onslaught lasted for one hour then, as suddenly as they had appeared, they disappeared.

For a few moments after they flew off no one moved--all ears were searching for the sound of the engines in case they returned, but they didn't. Then utter chaos reigned. While I quieted the senior students, attempting to say a prayer with them before sending them home, students of the junior school were tumbling out of the front door and windows, running wild, yelling, crying, and panicking. I shouted at them to stop or slow down, but no one heard me. The younger children were being trampled upon as everyone ran in every direction. It was as if they had all gone berserk.

I had no idea where or in what state of mind Sister Doris was, but I wanted to see my students off first before seeking her out. I warned them to stay close to the trees and bushes as they went home and sadly looked on as they departed. The heaviness in my heart told me that I was seeing them for the last time, and I wanted to burst into tears, but I had to be strong. I was trained to be a pillar of strength for others, wasn't I? Well, now was no time for me to cave in to human frailty, but why then did I feel so weak, so humanly helpless? Why could I do absolutely nothing as I watched the city of Greenville being shelled and my students scattering in every direction? I longed to crawl into a hole and give vent to the tears of helplessness, frustration, anger, and sadness that burned my eyes, but they would have to wait. There were more important and urgent matters to attend to.

In less than ten minutes the campus was empty. I ran over to the junior school and went in search of Sister Doris. Her classroom was the last in the building and I saw neither child nor teacher as I hurried there. When I walked into the room I was relieved to see Sister sitting on a desk among a group of her students and two of her teachers. These infants were either too little to walk by themselves or too scared to go home, and Sister did not want to leave them. I gently coaxed them to go on home quickly with the teachers who would take them. One boy, Sam, clung to Sister and bawled his head off, and I had to extricate him gently and hand him over to one of the teachers who was his aunt. I could see that Sister was badly shaken and I wanted us to get home as quickly as we could. I hadn't mentioned to Sister that we saw a bomb being dropped in the area of the convent.

Finally everyone left, and while Sister locked up the junior school I told her what we had seen. I told her that the port--and lord alone knew what else--was bombed out. Sister looked at me, both of us fearing the worst. We left the campus. As we turned off the main road and entered the back road to the convent, I remembered our passports. That meant that we had to go back into the main road. As we walked we beheld a scene of complete chaos. People were running in every direction, screaming and yelling, wild with fear. Young and old, men and women were hurrying along carrying bundles on their heads or their backs, dragging along young children and shouting at older ones following to walk faster and keep up the pace. The exodus had begun all over again and I somehow felt that it would be the last.

We went first to Vincent's house, but not a soul was in sight there. We then headed over to the courthouse. On the way we encountered the most gruesome sights. There were large craters in the roads and blood everywhere. After inquiring from people we met on the way we learned that the port was flattened, the hospital was hit, as well as several other buildings. Many people had been killed, including the chief doctor of the hospital. One man told us that he had seen Vincent going to the hospital to visit the wounded, so we headed over there. In the hospital there were pools and trails of blood everywhere we walked. Suddenly, I felt myself sway and realized that I was growing faint. I held the wall to steady myself, overcome by the harrowing experience I had lived through. I began to tremble and my stomach did somersaults so I signaled to Sister for us to leave. She agreed, and as we made our way to the convent we were expecting to encounter the worst.

Walking through the back road took us over an hour to reach the convent area and I was never so relieved as to see first, the clinic building, then the convent still standing and in one piece. There wasn't a soul in sight so we hurried up the path and as we entered the front door, called out to Sister Angela. She emerged from her room, visibly shaken but calm enough. Doris and I went to our rooms each convinced that we had taken enough. I for one wanted to get out and knew that Doris felt the same, because she had often expressed that desire.

I had begun undressing when I heard a loud banging on the front door. I quickly replaced my veil and went to answer the door. I recognized two hospital workers and I let them in. They were carrying a large carton which they nervously pushed into Sister Doris' hands as she came forward to greet them. I identified one as the person who had worked feverishly to save the mission boy, Simon. He explained that they were leaving the city but that the box contained over fifty thousand dollars, money collected from the thirteen or so clinics established throughout the county. They pleaded with us to take it into safe keeping and if we had to leave, would we please make sure and deliver it to Bishop Henry. I was hesitant about taking on such a responsibility in the midst of the war, but Sister Angela said we were obligated to help so she took charge of the box.

After the men left, Sister Doris opened the safe and took out all the school money that was kept there. I helped her count out teachers' salaries and place them in envelopes. We had planned to take the envelopes to the vice-principals of both schools to distribute when they met the other teachers. Since I had fewer teachers in the high school I was finished first and left her alone because I sensed she wanted to be alone. I took a cold bucket bath hoping it would calm my frazzled nerves and wash away the horrors of the morning we had just survived.

I was in the midst of a deep sleep when I was awakened by loud voices coming from the front of the house. I sat up confused. I checked my clock and saw that it was three o'clock in the afternoon, but the sun had already set and it looked more like six o'clock. The voices grew louder and more aggressive and so I hurried out to investigate. I was greeted by a group of heavily armed rebels, none of whom I recognized. Sister Angela stood blocking the front door while some of the rebels were trying to push past her and enter. I stood between her and the rebels and inquired what was wrong.

One soldier who identified himself as the chief, replied that they had come to remove our radio which they suspected we were using to transmit messages to the BBC and the United States. I repeated over and over that our radio had been long removed by another group of rebels. The skinny, foul- smelling rebel trying to push his way past Sister Angela became more insistent, declaring that he wanted to see for himself. I realized that the only way to convince them was to let them see the empty table outside my room where the radio had been previously kept. There was no point reasoning with that band of drunken, erratic ruffians.

About five rebels from the group surged into the corridor and then wandered from room to room. They poked at our beds with their guns, they ransacked our cupboards, rifling through our clothes and personal belongings. Then they spotted the wire. Along the wall outside Sister Doris's room ran a strip of wire that continued along the wall inside her room, the end of which hung idly behind her cupboard. Outside her window was a ground antennae, but it was not connected to the wire in her room. The evil-looking, skinny soldier went ballistic! He hollered to his companions who came rushing into Sister's room. He began jumping up and down exclaiming that they had caught the "spy." He began cursing Sister, verbally abusing her. He sneered at her and declared that her "American ass" would sleep in jail that night. As he did so he poked around some and came to one cupboard that was locked. He demanded that it be opened. Sister explained that it had always been locked, never opened. The rebel didn't buy that story and threatened to shoot the lock.

Sister said that she had a key from the school that might open it. I was scared because that was in fact the cupboard that camouflaged the safe, and I suspected that the rebel knew that. Someone must have tipped him off that we had enormous sums of money in safe-keeping. Sister went to her room and quickly returned with the key for the cupboard. She opened it but needed to go no further. The safe door was wide open and revealed a very empty safe. The rebel seemed disappointed. Sister Doris explained afterwards that she had only just finished counting up the money and hidden it in her room when the rebels arrived at the front door.

The rebels then decided to search Sister Angela's room. I saw her grow apprehensive, but she remained outwardly calm as though she had nothing to hide. When the ruffian espied several boxes under Sister's bed, he roughly demanded to know what was in them. Sister explained that they were filled with medicine for the clinic. She told him to open them if he wanted but he seemed to lose interest. He then turned and faced us and declared harshly that we were indeed spies and he was placing us under house arrest until we were marched down to the jail.

It was then I grew afraid. I felt a weak, tremulous feeling inside, but knew I couldn't give in, not now anyway. I knew full well what our fate would be once those bloodsucking, murderous villains got their hands on us. I would have preferred to take my life than suffer humiliation and torture by them. But I was determined not to die. I was too young and had not lived life fully nor as yet accomplished the goals I had set for myself, so I knew I had to find a way out for us.

The front door stood wide open and I edged my way unobserved toward it. The rebels paid me no mind as all their energies were concentrated on humiliating and threatening Sister Doris. As I reached the door, I realized that a small group of rebels were still out there standing around or sitting in a jeep they had no doubt stolen from someone. Then I saw in the distance three figures approaching. I clutched my rosary tightly, lunged out the door, and ran down the front path, despite the shouts from the rebels warning me to stop and return to the house.

I knew that our only chance was to seek help and I didn't care if I was shot in my attempt to reach those three men, whoever they were. I kept running, my chest feeling as if it would burst, until I came upon the three figures who turned out to be our two houseboys and Eddy, one of my students from the school. In between gasps for breath I shouted to the boys to go and find Malcolm, the general for the rebels in Greenville, or anyone whom they felt would help us. I warned them to be careful but to hurry. I then made my way back to the convent, but as I entered the door, one of the rebels remarked quite smugly that I was wasting my time because neither Malcolm nor Sakar, the second in command, nor any of my "friends" could help me because they were no longer in charge. I did not believe him but I was scared.

I made my way to the chapel and sat on the cold floor imploring God with all the strength left in me to save us from the hands of those men. After a few minutes I heard a vehicle approaching the convent and got up off the floor. I saw a jeep of soldiers but could not distinguish them. When the vehicle stopped in front of the convent, out jumped Malcolm, Sakar, my Lebanese friend, and several others of the rebels whom I had come to know. Malcolm spoke very gently to the ruffians who had intimidated us, assuring them that we were not spies but harmless women of God. He explained that he was the one who had removed our radio so they had nothing to fear from us. He tried to persuade them to leave us in peace, and all except the two dangerous-looking ones inside the house piled into their jeep and sped away. Sakar also pleaded with the two that had remained to go away and leave us be, but they didn't. Finally Malcolm, Sakar, and the others left.

The rebels that remained in the convent were bent on tormenting us. They ranted and raved, graphically describing what they would do to us now that we were in their clutches. I had to find a way out for us. I kept watching for the return of the three boys and when I saw them walking up the path I again went out and asked them to go and search for whoever in authority they could find to come and get the two rebels out of the convent, for night was fast approaching. They told me that they had seen an official from one of the logging companies driving into the house next to the convent so they would go and fetch him. I thanked them and returned to the chapel inside the convent.

About ten minutes later I saw the boys approaching with a man I did not recognize. I opened the door and let him in. Apparently the rebels knew him, and after talking, coaxing, and even pleading, Mr. Doe got those dogs out of the convent. Sisters Angela, Doris, and I were completely exhausted after that horrible ordeal, which was the last straw and sealed our determination to leave our mission in Greenville and go to a safer place. The task was now to procure a ride out of Greenville to Cape Palmas. After conferring with Bishop Henry, we would wend our way to the Ivory Coast, thus departing from Liberia never to return. We knew that the moment we were out of the convent, the rebels would step in, and destroy it, so even if we considered returning, we would have no house to which to return.

We kept the front door open so we could see anything that approached the path to the convent. While the three boys and I sat on the front steps and made plans to go to the town and look for any vehicle leaving the city, I saw a young man walking up the path. As he drew closer I recognized Rick, one of my students. I was more than happy to see him for one reason - he could find Vincent and recover our passports for us. His girlfriend was Vincent's daughter, and he practically lived with the family, so he would know their whereabouts. He greeted everyone and sadly announced that he and Vic, his girlfriend, were leaving the city. Since they didn't have a ride they were going to walk with a group of people along the beach until they reached the southeastern region of the country. I asked him to do me a big favor before he left and he replied, "Anything for you, Sis." I asked if he knew where Vincent was, and when he replied affirmatively, I begged him to find him and recover our passports. Rick was Clint's best friend and had become very loyal to me and also to the other sisters. I thus knew I could trust him to accomplish that task. About one hour later Rick returned with the precious documents. I thanked him profusely, gave him some money, and wished him well as I bid him an emotional farewell.

Sister Doris and I then set out for town in search of a ride out of Sinoe county while Sister Angela remained to pack whatever she thought we should take when we left. On our way we met a few teachers and told them to go to the school campus the next day to collect their salaries. We went to Sakar's house and he assured us that he would find a ride for us. He advised that we return to the safety of the convent and not worry. We returned to the convent and met Martin and Oliver, the two house-boys, cooking their rice on the coal pot in the convent. Eddy was with them, and they asked if he could stay with them because he also hoped to find a way out of Greenville. They informed me that Joseph, the Lebanese shopkeeper, was leaving that night and taking people in his new truck. They suggested that we go to his house and plead for seats on his truck.

The three boys accompanied me, and we could not believe the sight in front of Joseph's house. There were hundreds of people camped out in the street awaiting his appearance. People with suitcases, rice sacks stuffed with their precious belongings, cardboard cartons, and even mattresses were yelling, shouting, and talking excitedly. We managed to squeeze our way through and reach the high galvanize gate. I pulled at it and discovered it was open but when I entered his yard I was greeted by a scene that was almost funny at that point. The truck parked in the yard was packed to overflowing with people who had climbed over the gate or snuck in as I had. Joseph was standing on the tray attempting to get everyone off but of course no one budged. He screamed in all direction but no one heeded him. I was convinced that my quest there would be fruitless so I went back on the street and told the boys we should return to the convent.

The next day, Wednesday, March 24, 1993 is a day I will never forget. I awoke with a sense of foreboding. After our morning routine of prayer, Sister Doris asked me to accompany her to the school campus and with the three boys in tow we set out through the back road. We walked among the tall bushes just in case there was another air attack. We did hear the familiar drone of the jets but they were distant. Still, we hurried until we reached the campus. Sister went to the junior school and I to the senior. I didn't want to be there. I was overcome with a sadness that wanted to tear out my heart.

Two of the children whom I helped through school came to my office and I was happy to see them alive. I asked if they had seen Stanley, but they hadn't. In an effort to keep busy and shake off the sadness, I decided to conceal certain things in the roof of the building. I pulled down the hatch, the opening of which was in my office, and went up to survey the space. It was very spooky and hot like a steam house up there but it felt safe. Between the three of us we managed to pack the new typewriters I had recently purchased, the copy machine, musical instruments, a suitcase with my personal belongings, and two with Clint's things left with me when his family fled into their village in the bush.

The mission house was completed deserted. The two priests had left four mission boys there but they had all run away. I wandered around the yard and could see not even one of the numerous chickens the boys kept. Everything was silent and desolate; I had a great need to return to the convent. I walked over to the junior school and found sister in the book room stacking up the books from the shelves. "What's the use, Sis, you know that as soon as we leave people will come in and take everything," I said in despair. She said she had to keep busy doing something, otherwise she would go out of her mind. I understood how she felt, but I didn't have the energy she seemed to have nor the motivation to do anything other than search for a means out of Greenville. I suggested that we continue our quest, and soon we were heading out of the campus and across town.

Except for the occasional rebel cruising on the street, there was no one in sight. We passed homes that were completely deserted. Greenville City looked just like a scene out of an old western movie. We could not find anyone to ask who were the people killed by the bombs. After a few minutes walking in silence, Sister Doris declared that she was getting a bad dose of the "willies," so could we return to the convent. I was only too happy to oblige, because I was not feeling too well myself.

On the way to the convent there was a shop owned by some friends of mine. I knew that it had been closed when the people ran off after the bombing. As we neared it I could hear loud voices talking excitedly and even swearing, and I knew it had to be rebels. Sister Doris and I were scared and wanted to turn back and take another route to reach the convent but some of the men had spotted us and greeted us loudly, "Hey, lovely ladies, what brings you to these parts?" Martin, being a spunky young man and very protective of us, quickly jumped in front of us and answered, "They live here, Sir, and they are nuns not ladies!" I looked at Martin and smiled and wondered at the distinction he had just made. I strongly believed that the twenty-odd men sitting under the shop would be irrational and flying high. The air reeked of marijuana and alcohol. I looked to the side of the shop and saw a large truck camouflaged with branches parked in the yard, and my heart leaped with hope.

Whenever I wanted to get anyone's attention I had a particular way of clearing my throat, and I did that hoping to get Martin's attention. When he cast a glance my way I looked at him intently and threw my eyes in the direction of the truck. He blinked to signal that he had received my message. Sister Doris and I politely greeted the rebels and walked on while Martin, Oliver, and Eddy stayed back. Sister looked back when she realized that they had not followed us and made as if to call out to them, but I held her hand to stop her. When we had walked far out of sight and earshot of the rebels, I explained that I had seen a truck in the yard and I was sure that the boys had remained to negotiate a ride for us out of Greenville. As we neared the convent I squeezed my eyes tightly, made a fist, beat my breast, and cried, "Please God, let those men be our way out!"

I grew alarmed when some thirty minutes later I saw the three boys approaching the house accompanied by two of the rebels. I opened the door and stood on the front steps until the men were almost on top of me. I looked intently at Martin and raised one eyebrow in question. He immediately calmed my fears by smiling and nodding slightly to indicate that it was okay. "Sister, these men need to speak to you," Martin stated, and I invited them inside without hesitation. The men politely introduced themselves and I noticed that they spoke very proper English. I saw that they were not from Greenville, and their next statement confirmed that. They announced that they were from Gbarnga and had come to Greenville to bring ammunition for their men who had remained but would be returning that night. My spirits soared.

I turned to Carl, the one who had introduced himself as the commander, and bluntly asked, "Will you take us, sir?" I knew Martin had already explained our predicament and I was anxious to know their answer. "Yes, madam, we will take the three of you and your boys. All we need is some fuel, and you will have to pay," Carl replied. I could have embraced the dirty, foul-smelling man, so elated was my heart. Money would be no object and it so happened I had a drum of fuel hidden in a storeroom on the mission. I was sure that if we couldn't find the key we would be able to break the lock so I was delighted to reply, "I think we can meet your requirements. What time would you be picking us up?" The two men settled a time with us, shook our hands, and left. For a moment I thought I was going to faint with excitement. I could not believe that we would actually be leaving Greenville on our way out of Liberia!

The men left at 5:00 P.M. promising to return at 8:00 P.M. for us. We had three hours to obtain special passes to leave the city as well as perform other last-minute duties, so Doris and I set out for the police station. When we got there the few officers on duty informed us that only the chief could issue those passes and he was at that time performing the burial ceremony for the chief doctor from the hospital who had been killed in the bombing. Martin again came to our rescue and said that he would go and track him down. Oliver accompanied him while Eddy remained at the station with us. About thirty minutes later the boys returned with the police chief who readily performed the service we required. Of course he expected a monetary reward, and at that point I would have paid any sum for those passes.

After paying one hundred dollars and obtaining the necessary passes I wanted to go onto the mission to see if anyone was there who either had the keys to the room with the drum of fuel, or knew where we could get them. There is a saying that God never deserts his own, and that was never truer than that day. When we got to the mission we met two boys whose family lived on the port. When I asked them what they were doing there they told me that the mission boys had left the keys with them and they had just come to check that everything on the mission was safe. A few days ago I thought my heart was going to pop with fear, now I thought it would pop with joy. I took the keys from the boys, opened the storeroom and searched for the drum of fuel. There in the corner, just where I had placed it, sat the drum. I closed the door, replaced the lock, but did not lock it. Satisfied, I beckoned to Sister and the boys that we should go. I still had one more important chore to do.

Returning to the convent I went to my room and pulled out a box from behind my cupboard. In it I had hidden the school money and I wanted to give some of it to the teachers while the rest I would use to pay the rebels to get us out of Greenville. There was a group of young people quite unknown to me but who suddenly became extremely friendly and I realized that it was only because they wanted a ride on the truck. I didn't mind who else got on that truck once the three of us and the three boys who had stuck by us did. I quickly counted out half of the money, put it in a bag, and set out for the house of my vice- principal which was about a mile in back of the convent. Eddy saw me going alone and ran out to meet me. He asked where I was going and I told him, so he accompanied me.

I knew the gentleman I was going to visit was well loved by all the students. He was an exceptional teacher and a good man. He had been fortunate enough to have studied in England and was open-minded, intelligent, kind, and extremely patient with the students. When I got to his house his neighbor, who was also a teacher in the high school, informed me that Mr. King had stepped out but would be back soon. I decided to wait because I had to see him. About ten minutes later he returned and I spoke with him.

I praised him for all his good work, thanked him profusely for his support of and assistance, to me and especially the students for whom I knew he cared deeply. I handed him the bag of money which I asked that he distribute to the other teachers and then told him that everything was now in his hands. Instead of gloating over the praises I had just bestowed on him, I saw his shoulders sag and his eyes grow misty. He asked if we were going, and I said yes, then he asked if we were returning and I replied, "I very much doubt that!" I left then because I knew I was close to breaking down.

Returning to the convent I experienced a poignant sense of sadness and desolation. The sisters were busy packing as much as could fit into their suitcases. I went to my room and surveyed my one suitcase and overnight bag. I knew I was not returning to Liberia and I did not really care what I took with me. I had intended to begin a new life wherever fate took me. I brought my bags out and placed them close to the five that stood in the corridor. The "hospital" money was hidden in one while the sisters had two each. Ben was going to remain in the convent in an attempt to prevent the rebels from moving in when we left, but I was convinced that they would throw him out and move in anyway.

As darkness descended and swallowed us up, I was suddenly fired up by a sense of excitement and an urgency to get out of Greenville and Liberia. I kept my eyes tuned for the sound of the truck and soon enough I heard the sound and saw the glaring lights as it approached the convent. When it stopped in front our door, about twenty soldiers jumped out from every part of the truck. I immediately smelled the marijuana and the alcohol on them and steeled myself from the panic that was threatening. The soldiers placed our bags in the tray and the two sisters boarded the front of the truck.

Since there was no more room there for me, I began to climb up the tray and was helped on by one of the rebels. Martin quickly brought one of the cane chairs from the porch, and placing it in one corner of the tray, signaled me to be seated. I thanked him and placed on the hard seat one of the pillows I had taken from my room. I then covered myself with one of the blankets and passed around the rest to the boys so at least they would keep warm even if they were uncomfortable. I leaned over the side of the truck to ask if the sisters were comfortable and I saw two other soldiers squeezed into the front of the truck. I looked into the face of the one behind the wheel and then I panicked. His eyes were wide, glazed, unfocused, and bloodshot. He was really spaced out and flying high from too much marijuana and alcohol and I wondered just how far we would get that night with him driving.

As the truck drove off I reminded the commander who sat in the tray to stop on the mission for us to get the fuel. When we got there I told Martin and Oliver, who were seated around the chair, to go and bring out the drum. They asked if I had the key and I explained what I had done with the lock. The truck was refueled and about twenty more passengers had embarked before we drove off from the mission yard. One of those passengers was Mavis, a woman who lived close to the mission and who had become a good friend of mine. She was always busy making "market" so was known to possess large sums of money. She brought several children and young girls on the truck, each of whom I noticed carrying a stuffed animal toy. I wondered what she had done with all her money but didn't have to wonder for long. Mavis disclosed that she had stashed her money in the stuffed animals. So much for discretion!

Before the truck reached the first checkpoint, which was about ten miles from the mission, it made about ten stops to pick up passengers. People kept piling into the tray with luggage of different sizes and shapes. Two men came aboard with a mattress which they placed over the iron frame of the back of the truck. Several people then climbed up and made themselves comfortable on the mattress. Adults kept screaming at children to "make yourselves small" as they kept packing them into the truck like sardines. Martin, Oliver, and Eddy sat around my chair and "boxed" me in so that no one sat close enough to make me uncomfortable. I was too tired to really care but I was nonetheless touched by their protectiveness and thoughtfulness.

After the driver passed the checkpoint he drove for miles without stopping for anyone. I was familiar with the area we approached and I knew there was a broken, particularly dangerous bridge over a deep ditch. I began to wonder if the driver was capable of negotiating that bridge in his drunken stupor, when I heard the rebels in the front of the truck arguing loudly about who should take the wheel to cross the bridge. The driver did not surrender the wheel as the other men suggested. As we came near the bridge he stopped abruptly, accelerated, and then took off at a flying speed, but the truck did not get far. It lurched to one side, then to the other, then came to a stop as the wheel got caught in the space where a plank was missing. It lay precariously perched on its side as passengers scattered in every direction. The mattress at the top flew off into the ditch taking with it those who lay on it.

When I felt the first lurch I crouched down on my chair and held onto the bars on the side of the truck. I didn't go flying off but my chair was tilted on its side and I froze with fear. I slowly lifted my head but could see nothing in the darkness. The air was pierced by the frantic screams of children as well as adults. I sat up and looked for Martin, Oliver, and Eddy. I soon saw them lying on their sides and when I called out and asked if they were hurt they replied that they were not. So I enlisted their help to search out those who had been thrown off the truck. In the meantime, the rebels had pulled the driver off the truck and were beating the life out of him. They were using both their fists and their guns. I used all my strength and shouted with all my might for them to stop before they killed him, even though I wanted to do so myself. I made them pick him off the ground and place him in the back of the truck so that he could sleep off his drunkenness. People were rushing around picking up their belongings that were scattered all around. Those who were on the mattress were located in the ditch and were brought up. They were covered in blood from cuts and bruises and one had a large cut on his head. One little girl, the eight-year-old daughter of the police chief, was brought up from the ditch with a huge, gaping hole in one cheek. I began to tremble when I saw her cheekbone sticking out and several of the women began to wail. Mavis quickly removed her lappa and wrapped the child's face with it.

The injured were bandaged and given sedatives for their pain and everyone settled in once again. Another rebel took the wheel, but we had another scare when he attempted to drive the truck out of the hole in which it was stuck. It rocked and lurched, threatening to topple again. I spoke to the commander and suggested that some of his men get out and help push out the wheel. They did that and it worked. We drove without any hitches until we arrived at one of the logging camps. The driver decided that everyone should rest, so he parked the truck in the camp yard and promptly went to sleep. Everyone else just lay or sat where they were and dozed.

I must have slept because the next thing I knew I was awakened by a big commotion all around me. I checked on the sisters to make sure they were fine and then looked around to see what was happening. The boys informed me that we were about to resume our journey. I was glad because I wanted to get to Cape Palmas as soon as possible. The rebel behind the wheel was the only sober, sensible one at the time, so everyone cheered loudly when the commander suggested that he continue to drive. As he guided the truck out of the camp and onto the main dirt road, I sent a silent prayer up to God. He drove without stopping until we got to Pleebo. Everyone was hungry, thirsty, and wanted to go to the bathroom, but we exercised self-control so as not to delay the journey.

It was after 6:00 P.M. when we got to Pleebo, and if things went well at the checkpoint we should have been in Cape Palmas in another hour or so. But that was not to be. The rebel ruffians in Pleebo insisted that everyone disembark, especially the three sisters, so that they could check our passports. We did as they asked and went to the desk where the officials sat, but while I was making my way down from the tray of the truck in the darkness, I missed my footing and fell over six feet down flat on the concrete. I landed on my back and as I was helped up, my foot twisted and began to pain severely, but I paid it no mind.

The rebels took our passports and scrutinized them while asking a barrage of irrelevant questions. I was warned not to lose my cool, so I made every attempt to remain calm. The one who said that he was in charge ordered us to remove our luggage from the truck and open them piece by piece. My knees rattled violently and my heart beat so fast I thought it was going to pop out of my ribcage. I knew the sisters were apprehensive too because we had a suitcase filled with money that we had to deliver to Bishop Henry. I went first and opened my red bag, then my suitcase with its meager contents. Then Sister Doris followed. When I saw the actions that followed, I knew she had a plan up her sleeve.

Sister began throwing the contents of her suitcase as far as she could. As fast as she scattered them people around gathered them up, but she kept throwing items around. I realized that she was stalling for time, because the next suitcase in line was the one filled with money. Suddenly, I heard a familiar voice yell, "Leave the sisters alone!" I turned and saw David, a young man from Greenville walking toward the desk where we were being held. David worked with one of the logging companies and was my good friend. He was driving the port manager's car to the bishop's house when he saw the big commotion. When he stopped and inquired he was told of our plight so he immediately came to our rescue. He sternly announced to the rebels that the bishop had sent him to give us a ride to his house and would be very angry if he returned without us. The rebels grumbled but let us go. At least they still had some respect left for the head of the church!

The bishop showed no emotion nor made any comment after we told him our story and announced that we were leaving Liberia. He did not ask if we had money to purchase tickets, if we needed anything, nor even offer to have his driver take us to the ferry to get us across to the Ivory Coast. I was not in the least surprised. I knew the cold, hard-hearted man who was supposed to be a man of God was just being his ugly self. After dealing with him the few times I had to, I had seen through him and I suspected he knew it because he thereafter was cold and distant with me.

With the help of the local doctor we made our way across the river and found ourselves in Tabu, on the Ivory Coast. One of the priests working there came to give us a ride into the town. He took us to the convent of some French sisters who welcomed us with open arms. They gave us a hot meal then took Sisters Angela and Doris to the bus depot to purchase tickets to for Abidjan. The three of us realized that we planned to go our separate way and no one attempted to influence or force us to change course. Events had been happening too fast for me and I needed time to assimilate it all.

I also wanted to get to Monrovia to find Clint. I considered it an act of God that he was not in Greenville during the bombings. I had sent him to Monrovia to register the senior students to sit for the national examinations. I was determined that I was not going to abandon him to a hopeless future in a Liberia that had nothing to offer a young person with high hopes and dreams. I had promised God that if I could help one Liberian to be a better person then my mission to that country would not have been in vain.

I knew that my choice of Clint to be that person brought much jealousy, hatred, and caused me to be all but ostracized by the sisters and even by my friends and family, but no one was going to pressure me to choose otherwise. I knew he wanted that chance and I was confident that I could offer it to him. I was willing to sacrifice even my life to accomplish that feat. Obtaining a visa for Clint to enter the States proved a greater challenge than I had anticipated. We made three attempts before the embassy officials in Monrovia would grant the necessary stamp.

It was a Friday, Good Friday at that, and I was leaving Liberia and the African continent for good. As I boarded the plane in Abidjan, I looked over the horizon of the Ivory Coast to the place where Liberia lay. I could not believe that I was leaving it for good. That land had turned and twisted my life around, had matured me, had taught me about various aspects of life, about war and death, but also about love. I had entered Liberia a naive, ingenuous, trusting young woman, and five years later I was leaving as a woman whose eyes had been opened to the world in more ways than one. In that seemingly Godforsaken land, ravished by war and suffering caused by the greed for power and wealth, I had been educated in the school of life.

I firmly believed then that dreams did come true. I had vividly dreamed of Clint, had traveled hundreds of miles and met him, and he had become a significant part of my life. I was scared but I was ready to begin afresh. I looked forward to my new life with joyful anticipation.

CHAPTER TWELVE

In my efforts to begin a new life I pushed Liberia, the people, the war, the pain and suffering I had experienced, far out of my thoughts. But after a few months they surfaced in the form of nightmares. The horrible sound of the jets, the dropping of the bombs, the screams, the blood, the chaos began to haunt me. Worst of all I began to feel depressed and guilty about the people who had been left behind in the midst of the horror and carnage, and the ones who had escaped but were existing in deplorable environments in the refugee camps on the Ivory Coast. My only solace was found in prayer, and so pray steadily I did. After a few months I was able to cope, but I could not put Liberia out of my mind.

What haunted me the most were the scenes of children bearing arms. One day during my last trip to Monrovia I was walking on the street in Sinkor, the area where I always stayed, when I encountered a group of boys no older than nine or ten years of age. I was both astonished as well as saddened to see them carrying various forms of weapons ranging from the most sophisticated guns to makeshift weapons -- comprising water pistols, broomsticks, garden rakes, rolling pins, air filters, coke bottles, and even a powerless power drill. Looking into the eyes of these boys, self-assured, arrogant eyes, long robbed of anything resembling childhood innocence, was a chilling experience because I saw their hunger for blood, their innocence punctured by cruelty and their sense of not knowing what was going to happen next.

Commandos, or leaders of those "packs" were barely in their twenties and adopted war names like "No Mother, No Father," "Housebreaker," "Barbed Wire," and "Butt Naked" to name a

few. There was a tale circulating about the one who called himself "Butt Naked." It was reported that whenever he went to battle, he disrobed in the face of enemy fire as a sign of defiance
and invincibility and led a brigade of fighters who wore only
tennis shoes to do battle. Decapitation was most prevalent, and
dozens of heads in various stages of decomposition littered the
streets in Monrovia. Sometimes, when there was a truce or the
fighters were bored, they played soccer with the dried, fleshless
skulls which they would nonchalantly retrieve from the gutter or
the roadside.

In Liberia, there is a small town called "Smell No Taste."
One legend has it that the town was so named because of its
proximity to the Robertsfield International Airport. Many of the
students whom I taught in the high school in Greenville had relatives there and would excitedly look forward to spending vacations with them. On their return they would recount stories of
why the town was so named. Apparently locals would gaze
longingly at well-heeled passengers hopping on planes bound
for London, Paris, New York, and other far-off places. The
Liberians could only fantasize about making such journeys or
living such a lifestyle. They were close enough to smell but too
far to taste. The same can be said about peace in Liberia. Peace
has been a carrot dangled in front of Liberians' noses more than
thirteen times during the almost ten-year-old civil war.

Instead of "freedom for all," which is what "Liberia" means
and the reason why it was established in 1822, Liberia has
become a free-for-all, reduced to primal clashes among tribes,
randomly slaughtering each other with the machine guns and
other sophisticated weapons supplied by those bent on prolong-
ing the carnage. Calling the situation in modern Liberia a "civil
war" is crediting it with too much organization and purpose.

The reality is villagers slaughtered by tribal-based militias
that mark their territories with the skulls of their victims. The
situation has been addressed in various ways but nothing strate-
gic or concrete has ever been done by the outside world, espe-

cially the United States, to permanently end the carnage which to this day still rages. It rages because the various insurgents are allowed to continue the attacks and senseless killings without being brought to justice for the murderous crimes committed since 1989.

Ray Harper, leader of the National Patriotic Front of Liberia (NPFL), the main insurgent in the 1989 attack on Liberia and the horrendous events that followed, self-acclaimed president after President Doe was captured and brutally murdered, walks around with an interesting resume. In 1984, he was accused of embezzling almost one million dollars from the Liberian government. He fled the country and came to the United States, where after committing a "petty" crime, he was imprisoned in Massachusetts. While awaiting extradition to Liberia he managed to escape from jail and found his way back to Africa, settling in Sierra Leone, which borders Liberia. There, with assistance from countries like Libya and the Ivory Coast, he amassed troops and finally launched his attack on his own country, Liberia, on Christmas Eve, 1989.

The greed for power of this "Americo-Liberian" warlord led him to destroy the country he swore he would rule well. He is as guilty as his ill-trained and brutal "troops" of all the atrocities committed, not only in Monrovia but in the other parts of Liberia -- atrocities of which the larger world is not aware. He and his band of hoodlums killed the Catholic priest in Greenville, the five Catholic nuns in Garnersville, as well as hundreds of thousands of innocent civilians as they went on a rampage of slaughter that stretched from Monrovia to Cape Palmas. In his blind pursuit to rule the country, Harper made two attempts to capture Monrovia in 1990 and 1992, and when both were unsuccessful, politics took over and did what bullets couldn't. He was made a member of a ruling committee, but arrogance overtook reason, and he overstepped his authority several times, the last being when he attempted to arrest another insurgent for murder. How ironic! This murderer pointing a bold finger at another man, accusing him of crimes he himself had committed in droves!

Shortly after Harper launched his attack on the country, a six-nation West African peacekeeping force called the Economic Community of West African Cease-Fire Monitoring Group (ECOMOG) was deployed and essentially partitioned off Liberia into two zones. The first encompassed the capital, Monrovia, and was led initially by Arthur Sayer. The other half, run by Harper and his NPFL, amounts to about 96 percent of the country. What has occurred is that the outside world is only aware of Sayer's slice of the pie. It is the only area that is featured in any reports or remains the sole recipient of any aid from the world.

Harper never recognized Sayer as the interim ruler of Liberia. He proclaimed himself "President" Ray Harper with his wife of the moment, Rita, as First Lady, and made the town of Gbarnga his headquarters. After capturing one of the radio stations, he often addressed the nation and referred to Sayer and his cohorts as that "pack of Banjul manufactured morons!" - Banjul being the city where one of the many peace accords was signed and where Sayer was chosen to be the interim leader of Liberia until elections could be held. Reconciliation and peace agreements were proliferated, but Harper continually refused to attend any of those peace meetings. He in fact made a mockery of them by continuing to kill and plunder even as the ink was still wet on those accords.

In 1995 after Sayer had served two terms that saw immense sums of money being pumped into the city, he was relieved of his post. It was discovered that the funds intended to rebuild the country, had been diverted into the pockets of Sayer and his ministers. And while no charges were formally brought against Sayer, those in the know shook their heads in disgust when asked to name one good thing Sayer had done with all the monetary aid he received in the country's name while he was interim president.

The six-member interim council of state elected to rule the

country after Sayer proved just as ineffective as Sayer. Harper was one of the three warlords sitting on the council now led by Milton Sankar, civilian, author, and teacher who proved to be only a figurehead, a puppet controlled by Harper. When that council had served its purpose it was dissolved, and a female "president-designate" was appointed to rule the country pending free and fair elections.

No one can judge whether the loss of almost 200,000 lives and the regional devastation spawned by the Liberian crisis could have been prevented without extended military engagement by the United States, but it is difficult to find a Liberian who doubts that firm U.S. intervention would have made a decisive difference. Many United States officials agreed that more could have been achieved. The United Nations approved the ECOMOG operation established in 1991 and the secretary general said that such regional peacekeeping arrangements were the UN's preferred option for the future, since the big powers are increasingly reluctant to commit their forces. However, as I witnessed first-handed, ECOMOG soldiers acted as another faction in the conflict and were unable to stop the war in Liberia, even though they had been deployed there for over six years.

As I attempt to piece my life together I cannot seem to forget Liberia, this land that seems to have been forgotten by the rest of the world. Having become closely involved with a Liberian for the past years has made me more aware of the continuing carnage there and especially that those responsible are allowed to freely enjoy the luxuries of life. Recently, browsing through an African magazine, I was horrified to see photographs and a report of the lavish wedding of Mr. Ray Harper--the same Harper who raped Liberia, collected millions of dollars from the rubber and logging companies, led a pack of rogues, who murdered thousands of innocent civilians and even members of the church, foreigners whose blood was shed for the people whom they loved and left home to serve. The same Harper who was responsible for the deaths of so many people whom he conveniently "bumped off" when they dared to threaten him, challenge him, or stand in his way.

The five American nuns from Monrovia, the Ghanaian priest in Greenville, and many of the countless civilians killed by that man and his band of hooligans, were my friends, and my soul cries out to see justice done.

At the present time I am working in a family-owned company that encompasses several different businesses. I love my job as much as I love the people with whom I work. Because of all the unpleasant experiences I had, I had become suspicious of everyone. I receded behind a wall of coldness, aloofness, and seeming unfriendliness, which was a cover-up for my fear and pain. My normally cheerful, sweet, and patient disposition was marred by constant anger, and the gentle, warm, loving me was replaced by a toughness and a desire to hide away from everything and everyone.

At Cosmic, I was welcomed, and I soon felt a deep sense of "belonging." I was still extremely cautious and kept very much to myself, but not for long. Everyone in that office and even some of the men and women in the factory were so warm, friendly and helpful. I enjoyed giving my all and going the extra mile for customers and coworkers alike.

The office manager/comptroller, bookkeeper, quality control supervisor, building manager and I, were ironically all from non-American backgrounds. The multiplicity of our ethnic and cultural heritage enabled us to learn from and enrich each other's lives as we shared experiences. Working with the family members who own the company was the soothing balm I needed to heal the many wounds I had kept so carefully and tightly bandaged over the years.

As that warm, loving, generous, and extremely kind-hearted family reached out to people and did their part to enhance the lives of those less fortunate than themselves, they showed me that not all the rich and powerful were arrogant, snooty or mean as prior experiences had led me to believe. Unaware that their warmth, genuine interest, concern, and support for those around them have deeply touched me, they have helped me to thaw out the coldness that had enveloped my heart. I slowly regained my self-esteem and my faith in humankind as I was allowed to trust and share a special closeness with each of them.

I know not what the future holds for me, but I am filled with a profound sense of anticipation because, after all, "Thursday's Child has far to go!"

Thursday's Child

by
Sue Potter

Available at your locl bookstore or use this page to order.

--1-931633-14-2 - Thursday's Child - $13.25 U.S
Send to: Trident Media Inc.
             801 N. Pitt Street #123
             Alexandria, VA 22314
Toll Free # 1-877-874-6334
Please send me the items I have checked above. I am enclosing
$_____(please add #3.50 per book to cover postage and handling).
Send check, money order, or credit card:

Card #_____ Exp. date _____

Mr./Mrs./Ms._____
Address_____
City/State_____Zip_____

Please allow four to six weeks for delivery.
Prices and availabilty subject to change without notice.

Printed in the United Kingdom
by Lightning Source UK Ltd.
102565UKS00001B/37